MICROELECTRONICS AND MICROCOMPUTERS

Lionel Carter is a qualified Chartered Mechanical Engineer. He is Principal Lecturer in Management Science at Slough College of Higher Education. He has given lectures on computers, decision making and related topics at Birmingham University, Brunel University, Civil Service Staff College, EITB, Henley Staff College and the National Water Industry Council.

Eva Huzan is Head of the Computing Division at Slough College of Higher Education. Previously she worked as a physicist and computing lecturer in industry. She has carried out research in computing and physics at the London School of Economics and Political Science and at Queen Mary College, University of London, gaining PhD degrees in Solid State Physics and in Computing. She is a member of the Computing Science Advisory Panel ('O' and 'A' level), University of London, of the Advisory Committee for Mathematics including Computing, Southern Region Advisory Council, and of the ICL-CES (Computer Education in Schools) Advisory Panel, Southern Region, and is a committee member of the British Computer Society Microprocessor Specialist Group.

The authors have collaborated before in writing *A Practical Approach to Computer Simulation in Business* (1973), *The Pocket Calculator*, Teach Yourself Books (1979), and *Computer Programming in* BASIC, Teach Yourself Books (1981). They have also had a number of articles published in professional journals.

TEACH YOURSELF BOOKS

Microelectronics and Microcomputers

L. R. Carter M.Tech., C.Eng., M.I.Mech.E., M.B.C.S., F.O.R.
E. Huzan B.Sc., Ph.D.(Physics), Ph.D.(Computing), F.B.C.S.

Illustrated by G. Hartfield Illustrators

TEACH YOURSELF BOOKS
Hodder and Stoughton

First printed 1981
Second impression 1982

Copyright © 1981
L. R. Carter and E. Huzan

British Library Cataloguing in Publication Data
Carter, L.R.
Microelectronics and microcomputers. –
(Teach yourself books)
1. Microelectronics
2. Microcomputers
3. Microprocessors
I. Title   II. Huzan, E.
621.381′71 TK7874

ISBN 0 340 26830 1

Printed and bound in Great Britain
for Hodder and Stoughton Educational,
a division of Hodder and Stoughton Ltd,
Mill Road, Dunton Green, Sevenoaks, Kent,
by Richard Clay (The Chaucer Press) Ltd, Bungay, Suffolk.
Photoset by Rowland Phototypesetting Ltd,
Bury St Edmunds, Suffolk.

Contents

List of Figures

List of Tables

Introduction

This book has been written to give a basic understanding of microelectronics and microcomputers. It covers a variety of aspects at the introductory level including: microelectronic devices (chapter 1), number systems and logic circuits (chapters 2 and 3), microcomputer structure, functions, interfacing and data communications (chapters 4, 5, 6 and 9), programming (chapter 7), system development (chapter 8), and a range of applications. The applications include those dealing with aspects of instrumentation, industry, travel, leisure and the consumer industry, education and uses in the office (chapters 10–15).

The development of microtechnology has opened up the use of computers to many more people than was previously possible, and has changed the way many applications can be handled. In addition, the compactness and low cost of microcomputer-based systems are making possible new applications, where the versatility offered by a programmable device provides great flexibility for controlling equipment.

The business or scientific user, who may be using a microcomputer for the first time, needs to be aware of problems and procedures associated with the analysis, programming and running of data processing applications, including the use of software packages (supplied programs).

The engineer and scientist is increasingly expected to use microprocessor-based systems for recording measurements and controlling processes. These applications involve interfacing sensors, actuators and display units to microcomputers and require a knowledge of the types of microcomputing device available and how they may be linked.

The hobbyist, home and school user of microcomputers will find this book useful as background reading to the programs and applications given in microcomputing magazines.

1 Microelectronics

1.1 Development of microelectronic devices

Rapid development in technology depends often on two factors: the ability to produce large quantities of the product at the right cost; and a ready and expanding market for the product. The development of the transistor coincided with the wider use of digital computers in the late 1950s. There was a need to replace the valves used in computer circuits by smaller devices which used less power and were more reliable. The transistor fulfilled these requirements and assisted in the expansion of the use of computers in the 1960s, particularly for business purposes.

The development of microelectronic devices was not initiated by these business computer users. The need for very small electronic circuits of even greater reliability was established by organisations concerned with sending equipment into space, where the weight of the missile was a prime consideration. However, once the technology for fabricating microelectronic circuits was perfected, its potential use in the industrial and business sectors provided a huge new market for further exploitation.

Microelectronic devices (integrated circuits) are made from wafer-thin pieces of semi-conductor material, such as silicon. A small chip of silicon, a few millimetres square, can contain a very large number of electronic components built into circuits.

Integrated circuits (ICs) are available which have a wide variety of processing and storage functions. Today it is possible to have all the circuits needed for a micro-computer on a single semi-conductor chip, which is about the same size as the early ICs that contained only a few components. Large Scale Integrated circuits (LSI), containing many thousands of components, are now commonplace. Each integrated circuit (chip) is mounted in a package so that electrical connections can be made. The packages come in various shapes, a common one being the Dual In-Line Package (DIP) as shown in Figure 1.1.

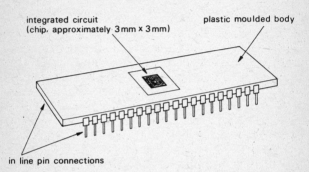

integrated circuit
(chip, approximately 3 mm × 3 mm)

plastic moulded body

in line pin connections

Figure 1.1   A Dual In-Line Package (DIP)

The availability of these small microelectronic devices allows the electromechanical devices in industrial and domestic equipment to be replaced by much more compact control systems, and has given rise to developments in automation which were not previously possible.

The use of microelectronic devices in computers has had a considerable effect in that computer power is now available in the office, on the shop floor, and in the home. These small, relatively inexpensive microcomputers can be used as stand-alone machines or may be linked to larger computers by means of communication links, such as the public switched telephone network, dedicated data lines and satellites. The larger central computers have also been reduced in size, and additionally have become more powerful and much less expensive by the use of microelectronic components in their construction. This trend is continuing with further improvements in the cost/performance ratio.

As the cost of microelectronic devices continues to fall, it can be expected that their use will become even more widespread.

1.2 Circuit elements

Valves, and then transistors, have been used in a variety of different circuits, for example, to amplify electronic signals and to generate radio waves. In computer circuits, one of the main uses of transistors is as a switching device.

Circuits consist of two types of components – those that are active such as valves and transistors, and those that are passive. In valve and transistor circuits, the components are said to be discrete as opposed to integrated. Discrete passive components include resistors, capacitors and inductors.

A discrete resistor may consist of a wire which has a high resistance or alternatively may be made of carbon. The moulded casing of the resistor is usually colour-coded for easy identification of its value. Resistance is measured in ohms (Ω) and values of discrete resistors can range from microhms ($10^{-6}\Omega$) to megohms ($10^{6}\Omega$). Resistors are used to restrict the flow of current in a circuit.

Capacitors are used in circuits for storing an electric charge. In their discrete form, capacitors consist of layers of good conducting material, such as metal, separated by an insulating material, such as air, waxed paper or mica. Usually many conducting and insulating layers are used to give capacitances measured in micro- (10^{-6}) or pico- (10^{-12}) farads (μF or pF).

An inductor may be made from a coil of wire. When a current is passed through the coil, a magnetic field is set up. The magnetic field is changed by changing the current. Energy may be stored in the magnetic field of the coil so that a coil may contain a current when a circuit is broken. This current can be discharged through a capacitor placed across the coil; the capacitor then stores the energy. Inductance is measured in henrys (H). A larger inductance may be achieved by placing an iron core inside the coil. Inductors are used in a variety of ways, e.g. as a choke to suppress fluctuations in rectified voltages. They are used in tuned circuits to select specified frequencies, and also in filter circuits.

Microelectronic circuits must have the active and passive circuit components built into the material (e.g. silicon) of which they are made. The physical properties of silicon only allow small values of resistance and capacitance to be formed, and no inductance. This is compensated for by the ability to build in large numbers of transistors.

1.3 Semi-conductor electronics

Materials can be classified as good conductors of electricity or bad conductors (insulators) or semi-conductors. Examples of semi-conductors are silicon, germanium and gallium arsenide, and these substances have been used to form transistors and microelectronic devices.

An atom of material consists of a nucleus surrounded by layers of electrons (negatively charged particles). The electrons in the outermost (valence) layer of an insulator fill that energy level. On the other hand, the valence layer of a conductor, such as copper, has a single electron which can readily migrate to another atom.

Materials such as silicon have four valence electrons. Neighbouring atoms share electrons with each other to form covalent bonding, which is a stable structure and hence makes pure silicon a poor conductor. However, it is possible to form semi-conductors by adding impurities to the pure silicon crystal. Two types of semi-conductor regions can be established in the material.

If the silicon is doped with a material having only three valence electrons (such as boron), then an area will be formed which has a missing electron (hole) and hence a positive charge (p-type region). Electricity is conducted in p-type semi-conductors by the propagation of these positively charged holes.

An extra electron (as opposed to a hole) is formed when silicon is doped with a material (such as phosphorus or arsenic) which has five valence electrons. The negatively charged regions thus formed are known as n-type semi-conductors.

A semi-conductor diode consists of a p-n junction, and allows electricity to flow in one direction only. This is achieved by applying a positive voltage to the p-side of the diode and a negative voltage to the n-side. Since like particles repel each other and oppositely charged particles attract each other, the effect is for holes in the p-type region to flow across the junction from p to n, and electrons from n to p. A resultant forward-biased current is produced which increases as the applied voltages are increased. The current is reduced to a very low value when the diode connections are reversed.

A diode may be used to rectify alternating currents, but it does not amplify currents. A current amplifier is made by adding another layer of doped silicon to form a transistor. The three layers are called the emitter (E), base (B) and collector (C), as shown in Figure 1.2. The base may be made of n-type material sandwiched between two layers of p-type material to form a p-n-p transistor, or of p-type material with n-type material for the emitter and collector (n-p-n transistor).

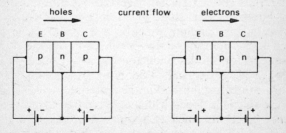

Figure 1.2 p-n-p and n-p-n transistors

In the p-n-p type of transistor, the emitter has a positive voltage applied to it, the base a small negative voltage and the collector a larger negative voltage. Holes flow across the junction from the emitter to the base. The latter is very thin so that most of the holes cross to the collector and a large current flows from the emitter to the collector, while only a small current flows in the base circuit. In this way, a large current flowing through the transistor can be controlled by the small current flowing through the base circuit. Similarly, in n-p-n transistors (p-type base), the current is carried by electrons.

These types of transistors are known as bipolar junction transistors, since they have two p-n junctions, and both electrons and holes are used in their operation. The field effect transistor (FET) uses only one p-n junction and only one type of carrier. It consists of a silicon bar with a channel of n- or p- type material through which the current passes from the source (S) to the drain (D) electrodes. A third electrode G (the gate) is placed at the centre of the transistor next to the p- region (for a n-channel transistor). A voltage (V_{DS}) is applied across the source and drain electrodes to cause current to flow from source to drain.

The flow of this current is restricted when a small negative voltage (V_{GS}) is applied to the gate electrode due to a small electrical field which is built up. This field gives rise to an area containing no free electrons (depletion region), see Figure 1.3. When the voltage on the gate is increased (i.e. made more negative), the depletion region extends across the channel until at the 'pinch-off' point no current can flow between source and drain. The action of the FET is analogous to that of the triode valve, and the gate performs the function of the grid in the valve. Amplification of the current flowing through the transistor from the source (valve anode) to the drain (valve cathode) can be controlled by small changes in the voltage on the gate.

The gate does not need to be in direct contact with the semi-conductor channel. In MOSFETS (metal-oxide-semi-

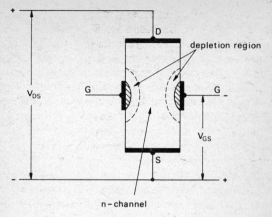

Figure 1.3 An n-channel FET showing depletion region

conductor FETs), the gate is insulated from the semi-conductor by a thin layer of silicon oxide. This gives a very high gate-channel resistance and allows this type of transistor to be used in circuits containing high impedance devices.

The above examples are typical of the most commonly used devices in microelectronics. Many other types of specialised solid state device exist such as transistors used for detecting or emitting light. When light falls on the semi-conductor junction of a phototransistor (or photo-diode), the effect is to increase the total current flowing. A light-emitting diode (LED), on the other hand, causes light to be output when electrons and holes collide and lose their energy. A red display is given out by LEDs made from gallium arsenide.

1.4 Fabrication of integrated circuits

A microelectronic circuit may contain many thousands of components and these need to be fabricated by the combination of a number of techniques. The complete circuit may comprise many layers of semi-conductor material (e.g. silicon) separated by insulating material (e.g. silicon dioxide). Each layer has its pattern engraved on it and this is etched into the insulating material by a masking process known as photolithography.

Microelectronic components are created by introducing impurities (dopants) selectively into the semi-conductor substrate. The required n- or p- type regions may be obtained by diffusing layers of the dopant into the substrate by heat treatment. Control needs to be achieved of the amount of impurity as well as its position.

Impurities can also be introduced under controlled conditions by means of ion implantation techniques. The atoms of the dopant are ionised so that they have the correct amount of energy. The semi-conductor wafer is masked so that only the exposed area will be penetrated by the energised particles of the dopant.

Further thin films of semi-conductor and insulating material are deposited on the layers by a variety of techniques. In addition, a layer of metallic conducting material is required to which electrical connections will be made. Many individual chips are manufactured at one time on a larger wafer, and each circuit must be tested before the good circuits can be bonded into protective packages. In the last stage, electrodes are connected to the circuits and final testing is carried out.

1.5   Microelectronic components

Microelectronic transistors

Microelectronic transistors are made by creating layers and islands of the appropriate p- and n- type material in the semi-conductor chip. Both bipolar and MOSFET transistors can be fabricated. The latter are called n-MOS or p-MOS depending on whether electrons or holes are used as the active carriers.

Some applications require low power consumption circuits as well as speed. This is achieved by CMOS (complementary MOS) circuitry. Although several transistors are contained in the circuit, the power consumption is low. This is because the number of transistors that are conducting electricity is reduced to one when the circuit is not performing the switching function.

Fabrication technology has advanced rapidly. Techniques have been developed which give much improved packing densities (the number of components that can be contained per mm^2 of semi-conductor chip) and greater speeds. High performance is achieved by three types of MOS technology

Silicon on Sapphire (SOS) is the fastest but requires an expensive substrate. CMOS/SOS chips are used in some computers because of their low power/high heat dissipation characteristics.

V-MOS technology achieves high densities by using a three-dimensional structure for each transistor in a chip, with the channel laid along V-shaped grooves. Fast speeds are obtained, however, the fabrication method tends to be more expensive than that used for H-MOS chips.

H-MOS technology saves space by reducing the size of the structures that are used in conventional planar n-MOS chips, and also achieves high performance.

Additionally, gallium arsenide circuits have been developed for applications requiring very fast speeds.

Resistors and capacitors

The fabrication of transistors into microelectronic circuits, although requiring high technology, does not present a fundamental difficulty. The fabrication of passive elements to match those found as discrete components in conventional circuitry is more difficult to achieve, and in some cases impossible.

Microelectronic resistors may be fabricated from thin sections of p-type material maintained at a negative potential with respect to a larger n-type region in which they are imbedded. This will cause only a reverse current to flow across the junction. Large values cannot be obtained and it is difficult to obtain precise values. However, because the cost of fabricating a microelectronic transistor element is similar to that for a resistor element, it is possible to use a transistor instead of a resistor. The resistance can be set by controlling the voltage or current applied to the transistor circuit.

A microelectronic capacitor can be formed by a thin layer of insulating material, such as silicon dioxide, sandwiched between a layer of heavily-doped semiconductor material (conductor) and a layer of aluminium (second conductor). The values of capacitance achieved are very small.

With present technology it is not possible to fabricate microelectronic inductors. However, capacitors and inductors can often be replaced by a circuit of microelectronic transistors; this applies particularly to digital logic circuits such as those used in microcomputer systems where only two values of the signals (high or low) need to be recognised.

1.6   Microcomputer systems

Microcomputer systems can be constructed from a number of different integrated circuits. The ICs are mounted on a printed circuit board (PCB), so that they can be connected easily to each other and other components, including discrete resistors, capacitors and transformers to enable power supplies to be linked.

Many systems are designed to have a modular structure, so that different micromodules can be combined for different applications. The systems range from very small units, which can be built into machinery, to complete systems with facilities for transferring information into and out of the microcomputer. The latter can have sufficient storage and processing capabilities to enable it to be used for commercial and scientific data processing applications.

2 Number Systems

2.1 Binary representation

As we have seen in Chapter 1, section 1.5, digital logic circuits require just two levels of signal, high or low voltage. Using binary notation, a high voltage can be used to represent a binary digit (bit) whose value is 1, and a low voltage to represent a 0.

Different combinations of 1s and 0s may be used to represent numbers and characters (letters of the alphabet and special characters). It is possible to carry out arithmetic operations on binary numbers in a similar way to that used for decimal numbers. Digital logic circuits can be built which store numbers in binary form, and others which can perform arithmetic operations on the stored numbers.

Many computers use groups of eight binary digits for encoding characters (see Appendix B for ASCII code). A group of eight bits is called a byte. For simplicity, we will start by considering groups of four bits only for binary arithmetic operations.

We know the value that a decimal number represents by virtue of the positions of the decimal digits. The position of each digit shows which power of 10 it should be multiplied by. For example, the number 8527 is equal to:

$$8 \times 10^3 + 5 \times 10^2 + 2 \times 10^1 + 7 \times 10^0$$

Remember that any number raised to the power 0 is equal to 1.

Binary numbers are represented in a similar way, but the binary digits (0 or 1) are multiplied by the appropriate power of 2. For example, decimal 13 (13_{10}) is represented by the following binary pattern:

1101

since $1 \times 2^3 + 1 \times 2^2 + 0 \times 2^1 + 1 \times 2^0 = 13_{10}$

That is, $13_{10} = 1101_2$

The maximum decimal number that can be represented by four bits is 15_{10} (1111_2). For larger numbers extra bit positions need to be used. For example,

$$10101_2 = 1 \times 2^4 + 1 \times 2^2 + 1 \times 2^0 = 21_{10}$$

Decimal to binary conversion

To convert from decimal to binary, we divide the decimal number successively by 2 giving a remainder of 0 or 1 at each stage. The binary number is given by the digits in the remainder. 21_{10} may be converted to binary by successive division by 2 as shown in the following example:

5	4	3	2	1	step
2	2	2	2	2	divisor
1	2	5	10	21	decimal number
1	0	1	0	1	remainder (required binary number)

Exercises

1 Convert 1011_2, 0101_2, 110010_2, 010111_2, 10111010_2, to decimal numbers.

2 Convert 24_{10}, 31_{10}, 78_{10}, 159_{10}, to binary numbers.

The answers are given in Appendix A.

Rules for binary addition

The rules for binary addition are:

1 Two 0s added together results in a 0, i.e. $0 + 0 = 0$.
2 0 and 1 (or 1 and 0) added together results in a 1, i.e. $0 + 1 = 1$ or $1 + 0 = 1$.

3   Two 1s added together results in 10, where the 1 is carried over to the next column, i.e. $1 + 1 = 10$.
4   Rules 1 to 3 are applied when adding more than two bits together. The next bit is added to the sum of the last two bits, i.e. $1 + 1 + 1 = 11$ and $1 + 0 + 1 = 10$.

$$\begin{array}{r} \text{For example:} \quad 101100 \\ +\ 110101 \\ \hline 1100001 \\ \hline \end{array}$$

The result of the first (right-most) column addition is 1 and that of the second column is 0. However, in the third column there are two 1s giving 0, carry 1. The fourth column has 1 and 0 giving 1, but there is a carry 1 from the third column addition, giving 0 and carry 1; this carry again gives 0 and carry 1 for the fifth column. The sixth column has two 1s and a carry 1 from the fifth column, resulting in 1 and carry 1 to the seventh column.

We can check the binary addition by converting the binary numbers to decimal, i.e.

$$101100_2 = 44_{10}$$
$$110101_2 = 53_{10}$$
$$\text{add} = 97_{10} = 1100001_2$$

Signed binary numbers

So far we have considered only positive binary numbers by ignoring the sign. We could just add the sign in front of the binary pattern as a 0 for $+$ and 1 for $-$. However, the processing of this representation of signed binary numbers is difficult to implement on electronic and electromechanical equipment as used in computers. Most computers use a different code, called twos complement, which requires less hardware.

The ones complement of a number is formed by replacing 0 digits with 1 digits and vice versa. For example, the ones complement of 0101 is 1010.

The twos complement is found by adding 1 to the ones complement, i.e. the twos complement of 0101 is 1010 + 1 = 1011. A quick way of finding the twos complement of a binary number is to replace all the 1s by 0s and 0s by 1s, working from left to right, until the final 1 (right-most) is encountered; this final 1 and the remaining digits to the right of it remain as in the original binary number.

Signed binary numbers have the left-most (most significant) bit set to 0 for positive numbers and to 1 for negative numbers. The negative value of a binary number is found by forming its twos complement. This means that the same hardware devices may be used for addition and subtraction, since to subtract a binary number from another one it is only necessary to change its sign by twos complement.

Binary arithmetic

The following examples show how signed binary numbers may be added or subtracted using the rules for binary addition, but dropping the final carry for twos complement operations. The arithmetic operations to be performed are:

$$5_{10} + 3_{10} = 8_{10}$$
$$5_{10} - 3_{10} = 5_{10} + (-3_{10}) = 2_{10}$$
$$3_{10} - 5_{10} = 3_{10} + (-5_{10}) = -2_{10}$$
$$-3_{10} - 5_{10} = -3_{10} + (-5_{10}) = -8_{10}$$

binary	*decimal*	*binary*	*decimal*
0101	5	0101	5
+ 0011	+ 3	+ 1101	+ (−3)
1000	8	(1) 0010	2

↑
final
carry
dropped

binary	*decimal*	*binary*	*decimal*
0011	3	1101	−3
+ 1011	+ (−5)	+ 1011	+ (−5)
1110	−2	1000	−8

↑
sign bit
will be 1

Note: The 8-bit representation of -8_{10} is 11111000_2

Exercises

3   Perform the following arithmetic operations in binary:

$$7_{10} + 4_{10}$$
$$7_{10} - 4_{10}$$
$$4_{10} - 7_{10}$$
$$-4_{10} - 7_{10}$$

The answers are given in Appendix A.

Binary fractions

Numbers can also be represented as binary fractions. In this case, the binary digits to the right of the binary point have corresponding values according to their positions as follows:

decimal point	*1st position*	*2nd*	*3rd*	*etc.*	
	2^{-1}	2^{-2}	2^{-3}		power of 2
	$\frac{1}{2}$	$\frac{1}{4}$	$\frac{1}{8}$		decimal fraction

The decimal equivalent of
1011.011
is $8 + 2 + 1 + .25 + .125 = 11.375_{10}$

Conversion from decimal to binary is carried out in a similar way to that used for integer decimal to binary conversion, but the digits to the right of the decimal point are multiplied by 2 as follows:

$$
\begin{array}{lll}
 & & carry \\
.375 \times 2 = 0.75 & \text{i.e. } 0.75 & 0 \\
.75 \ \times 2 = 1.5 & \text{i.e. } 0.5 & 1 \\
.5 \ \ \times 2 = 1.0 & \text{i.e. } 0 & 1 \\
\end{array}
$$

The carry gives the binary fraction .011 as shown.

Exercises

4 Convert 10100.011_2 to decimal.

5 Convert 9.75_{10} to binary.

The answers are given in Appendix A.

2.2 Binary coded decimal

Decimal numbers may be coded using binary digits, each decimal digit being represented by four bits. This form of number representation is known as Binary Coded Decimal (BCD).

For example, to represent 3685_{10} in BCD, we simply convert each digit to four bits as follows:

$$
\begin{array}{ccccc}
3 & 6 & 8 & 5 & \text{decimal} \\
0011 & 0110 & 1000 & 0101 & \text{BCD}
\end{array}
$$

i.e. $3685_{10} = 0011 \quad 0110 \quad 1000 \quad 0101_{BCD}$

Conversion from BCD to decimal is carried out by dividing the BCD number up into 4-bit units (nibbles) and then converting each nibble to a single decimal digit.

Exercises

6 Convert 6237_{10} into BCD.

7 Convert $0001 \quad 0101 \quad 1000 \quad 0011_{BCD}$ into decimal.

The answers are given in Appendix A.

2.3   Hexadecimal and octal numbers

We can avoid using the lengthy binary notation for numbers by converting binary numbers to a different code.

Hexadecimal codes are commonly used with microcomputers. The hexadecimal equivalent of a binary number is obtained by first dividing the binary digits up into groups of four, and then converting each group to base 16.

The hexadecimal digits corresponding to decimal 0 through 15 are 0 through 9 and A, B, C, D, E, F, that is $15_{10} = F_{16}$. For example, the binary number

$$10100111_2 = A7_{16} = 167_{10}.$$

Negative hexadecimal numbers are obtained by converting the twos complement of the binary equivalent. For example, -79_{10} is represented by 10110001_2 in twos complement form and this converts to $B1_{16}$.

Similarly, octal representation may be used in which numbers are converted to base 8. In this case, the binary digits are divided up into groups of three, and each group is represented by one of the digits 0 through 7. For example, using the binary representation of 167_{10} as before, we have:

$$010 \quad 100 \quad 111_2 \quad = \quad 247_8$$

Appendix C gives a table of decimal, binary, hexadecimal and octal numbers.

Exercises

8   Write down the hexadecimal representation of -38_{10}.

9   Write down the octal representation of 275_{10}.

The answers are given in Appendix A.

3 Logic Circuits

3.1 Boolean operators

Logical decisions may be defined using bits 1 and 0 to represent the on and off states, or high and low voltages, in logic circuits.

Boolean algebra is a two-state symbolic algebra which combines two bits (the input signals) by means of Boolean operators to produce a 1-bit output signal. Boolean algebra is used extensively in the analysis of logic circuits to determine the output from circuits which perform the functions of the Boolean operators.

The output signals from all possible combinations of the input signals are shown in Truth Tables. The name derives from the original use of Boolean algebra for determining the truth or falsity of propositions.

The OR operator

The Boolean algebra symbol for OR is $+$; this is not the same as binary addition. We will represent the two input signals by A and B.

The Truth Table for the OR operation is given in Table 3.1. This shows that the output signal is 1 only if A or B, or both are equal to 1.

The AND operator

The AND operator is represented by a multiplication sign (.). The Truth Table for this operation is given in Table 3.2. This shows that the output signal is 1 only if A and B are both 1.

| Inputs | | Output |
A	B	
0	0	0
0	1	1
1	1	1
1	1	1

Table 3.1   Truth table for OR operation

| Inputs | | Output |
A	B	
0	0	0
0	1	0
1	0	0
1	1	1

Table 3.2   Truth table for AND operation

*The exclusive-*OR *operator*

The exclusive-OR (XOR) operator is represented by the symbol $\oplus$. The Truth Table for this operation is given in Table 3.3. Notice that XOR allows us to detect if the two input signals are different (output 1) or the same (output 0).

| Inputs | | Output |
A	B	
0	0	0
0	1	1
1	0	1
1	1	0

Table 3.3   Truth table for XOR operation

The NOT *operator*

The NOT operator is different from the other three operators described, since it is not used to combine input signals but to invert a single input signal, i.e. the output signal from NOT A is 0 if A is 1 and 1 if A is 0. The operator is represented by a bar over the input symbol. For example, if A is 1

$$\bar{A} = \bar{1} = 0$$

3.2 Logic gates

A logic gate consists of a circuit with one or more input signals of high or low voltage, which produces *one* output signal. The latter will be a high or low voltage depending on the type of gate and the nature of the input signals.

Each type of gate may be represented by a standard symbol on a logic diagram. The following sections give examples of the different gates that may be used in logic circuits.

The Inverter (NOT gate)

The logic symbol for an inverter is shown in Figure 3.1. Remember that a NOT gate just inverts the input signal. We shall see later how this gate may be used in circuits where the *complement* of the input signal is required.

The OR gate

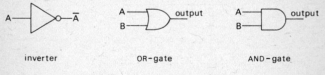

inverter   OR-gate   AND-gate

Figure 3.1 Logic symbols

The logic symbol for a 2-bit (diode) OR gate is shown in Figure 3.1. 3-bit, 4-bit etc. OR gates may be constructed by adding a diode for each extra input signal. The Truth Table for a 3-bit OR gate is given in Table 3.4. If any of the input signals (A, B or C) is a high voltage then the output is high.

The AND gate

The logic symbol for a 2-bit AND gate is shown in Figure 3.1. The AND gate may have two or more inputs and gives high output only when all input signals have a high voltage. This is illustrated in Table 3.4, which shows the Truth Table for a 3-bit AND gate.

Inputs			OR-gate	AND-gate
A	B	C	output	output
0	0	0	0	0
0	0	1	1	0
0	1	0	1	0
0	1	1	1	0
1	0	0	1	0
1	0	1	1	0
1	1	0	1	0
1	1	1	1	1

Table 3.4 Truth table for 3-bit OR and AND gates

3.3 Encoders and decoders

Two types of circuits that are commonly used in computers are encoders and decoders. An encoder may be used to convert input signals representing decimal values to their equivalent binary representation. A binary to decimal decoder converts binary numbers back to decimal.

A decimal to binary encoder

For simplicity, Figure 3.2 shows a circuit for converting only the four decimal numbers 0 through 3 to their binary equivalents. Switches are used to select any one of the four decimal numbers. We require two bits to represent the

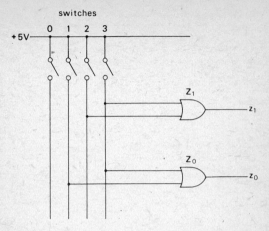

Figure 3.2 Logic circuit for decimal to binary encoder

decimal numbers 0, 1, 2 and 3, that is, 00, 01, 10 and 11. Therefore two OR gates are necessary; larger decimal numbers can be encoded by using more OR gates. Three OR gates will allow decimal 0 through 7 to be encoded; four OR gates can be used to encode decimal 0 through 15.

A high voltage (5v) on any input line to an OR gate will give a high output (a 1). For example, when switch 2 is closed, only Z_1 has a high input and hence high output, resulting in $z_1 z_0$ having the values 10 which is the binary representation of decimal 2. Table 3.5 gives the output from the two OR gates when each of the switches is pressed in turn.

switch on	Output from OR-gates	
	z_1	z_0
0	0	0
1	0	1
2	1	0
3	1	1

Table 3.5 Output from encoder

A binary to decimal decoder

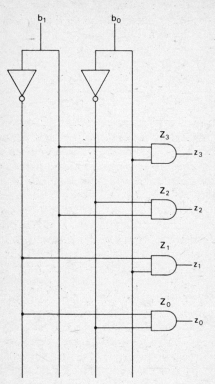

stored binary number

Figure 3.3   Logic circuit for binary to decimal decoder

Figure 3.3 shows a circuit to decode a 2-bit number into decimal. Each of the outputs z_0, z_1, z_2 and z_3 will be high only if *both* inputs to their respective AND gates are high. There are two signals output from the stored binary number, b_0 and b_1. These signals are each connected directly, and through an inverter, to the appropriate AND gates as shown.

When z_3 is high, this must indicate that $b_0 b_1$ is 11. To achieve this the b_0 and b_1 signals are connected directly to the Z_3 AND gate. z_2 must only be high when b_1 is 1 and b_0 is 0, that is, b_0 needs to be inverted so that it is changed to 1 before being input to the Z_2 gate.

The number of AND gates need to be increased for decoding larger binary numbers.

3.4   Parity testing

As mentioned in chapter 2, section 2.1, groups of eight binary digits can be used to represent numbers and characters as in the ASCII code. When these bytes of information are transferred from one device to another, mechanical or electronic errors may occur which cause one or more bits in the byte to be transmitted wrongly, e.g. a 0 is transmitted instead of a 1 in one or more positions within the byte. Each receiving or storage device can be designed to incorporate circuits for testing that each byte or group of bytes has an even number of 1s (even parity) or odd number of 1s (odd parity). This provides a means of checking whether one bit has been changed due to an error during the transfer process.

For example, some computers store information in groups of sixteen bits. A seventeenth bit (parity bit) may be added to each 16-bit word to give, say, odd parity. That is, if the information stored in the 16-bit word has a binary pattern containing an even number of 1s then the parity bit will be set to 1 to make the total number of bits in the 17-bit word odd. Conversely, if the encoded information in the sixteen bits has an odd number of 1s the parity bit will be set to 0.

When a word is fetched from the store its parity is tested. If the system is using odd parity then any word detected as having an even number of 1s will have a parity error, i.e. at least one bit must have been changed during transfer.

If two bits in the word have been changed then the

effect is cancelled out so that the word still has the correct parity and the errors will go undetected. Although this can happen, the probability is small compared with one bit being transferred wrongly. Other methods may be used to detect errors in more than one bit.

XOR *gates*

Exclusive-OR (XOR) gates may be used as parity testers. If an odd-parity word (odd number of 1s) is input to an XOR gate, as shown in Figure 3.4, then the output is high.

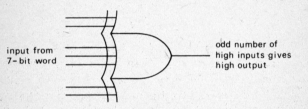

input from
7-bit word

odd number of
high inputs gives
high output

Figure 3.4   Odd parity tester

In an odd-parity system, a parity error is indicated if the output from the XOR gate is low.

3.5   Word comparators

Computers need to be able to compare two stored words to test whether they are equal or not. This can be achieved with exclusive-NOR (XNOR) gates, which are equivalent to XOR gates followed by inverters. The output from an XNOR gate is high if the inputs are the same.

For example, Figure 3.5 shows a circuit to compare two 4-bit words. If the bits in corresponding positions in both words are equal then the output of the XNOR gate receiving these two signals is high. The outputs from all the XNOR gates are fed into an AND gate. The latter has a high output only if all the outputs from the XNOR gates are high, i.e. the two words are equal. If one or more XNOR gates have a

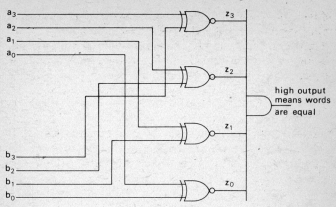

Figure 3.5 Comparison of two 4-bit words

low output the AND gate output will be low and the computer will have detected that the two bit-patterns are not the same.

3.6 Binary adders and subtractors

Section 2.1 in chapter 2 dealt with binary arithmetic; we will now look at some circuits which may be used to add and subtract binary numbers.

Half adders

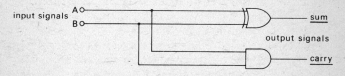

Figure 3.6 Half adder circuit

The logic circuit shown in Figure 3.6 is known as a half adder. This adds two bits (signals A and B) and outputs a *sum* and *carry* signal. Table 3.6 shows the Truth Table for this half adder circuit.

| Input signals | | Output signals | |
A	B	*sum*	*carry*
0	0	0	0
0	1	1	0
1	0	1	0
1	1	0	1

Table 3.6   Truth table for half adder

Full adders

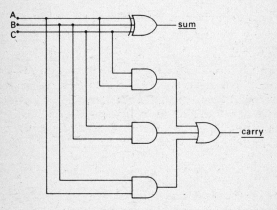

Figure 3.7   Full adder circuit

A full adder is needed to add three bits together as shown in Figure 3.7. The *sum* and *carry* outputs can be expressed as Boolean equations:

$$sum = A \oplus B \oplus C$$

where $\oplus$ means XOR addition so that *sum* is only 1 if there is an odd number of 1s.

Similarly,

$$carry = AB + AC + BC$$

that is, *carry* equals AB OR AC OR BC so that *carry* is 1 when two or more inputs are 1.

Note: AB means A AND B, AC means A AND C, BC means B AND C.

Exercise

10 Construct a Truth Table for the full adder circuit and check that the *sum* and *carry* outputs for each combination of input signals (A, B and C) give the correct binary addition.

The answer is given in Appendix A.

Binary adders

Figure 3.8 shows how two binary numbers may be added together. The right-most bits of each number, a_0 and b_0, are used as inputs to a half adder, and bits 1 to 3 of each of the numbers are input to full adders. Each full adder has an additional input signal which is the carry from the previous adder.

Exercise

11 Construct a Truth Table showing the inputs to the three full adders and their outputs, when the circuit in Figure 3.8 is used to add 7_{10} and 11_{10}. The answer to the addition is given by the *sum* outputs and the *carry* output from the final full adder. The *sum* output from the half adder (s_0) gives the right-most bit of the addition.

The answer is given in Appendix A.

Note: Binary adders for larger numbers are constructed by adding more full adders.

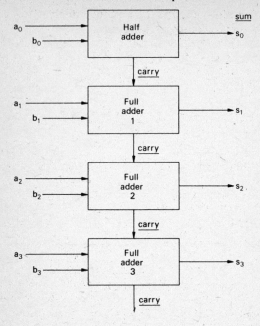

Figure 3.8   Addition of two binary numbers

Twos complement adder/subtractor

The twos complement number code was introduced in chapter 2, for adding and subtracting signed binary numbers. Figure 3.9 shows the logic circuit for a twos complement adder/subtractor for adding or subtracting two 4-bit signed binary numbers. Larger numbers may be added or subtracted by increasing the number of adders and XOR gates.

The XOR gates act as controlled inverters. When the invert signal (*subtract*) is low then the output from each XOR gate is equal to the b bits input to it. When the *subtract* signal is high the b inputs are inverted by the XOR gates; a 1 is also added to the first full adder, in this case, to give the twos complement of b.

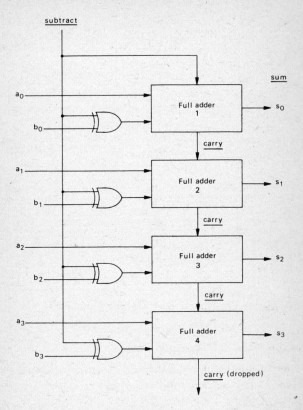

Figure 3.9 Logic circuit for twos complement adder/subtractor

This means that the circuit in Figure 3.9 outputs the algebraic *sum* of the two binary numbers ($a_3a_2a_1a_0$ and $b_3b_2b_1b_0$) when the *subtract* signal is low and the algebraic *difference* when the subtract signal is high. The final carry of the twos complement adder/subtractor is not used.

Exercise

12   Check that the circuit shown in Figure 3.9 produces
     the correct answers for the signed binary number
     arithmetic examples given in chapter 2.

3.7   Microelectronic implementation of logic circuits

So far in this chapter we have considered only logic
circuits. Each type of logic circuit may be implemented as
a microelectronic circuit using microelectronic transistors
and resistors.

The actual implementation depends on the type of
semi-conductor technology used, and on requirements
related to the use of the microelectronic circuits.

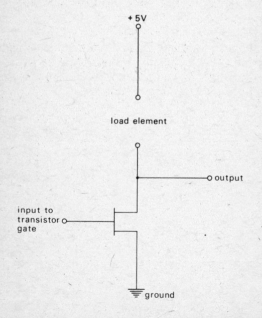

Figure 3.10   Electronic circuit for an inverter gate

For example, an inverter may be constructed using an n-MOS transistor and a load element in series. The load element limits the current flowing through the transistor when the supply voltage is applied, as shown in Figure 3.10. The input signal is applied to the gate of the transistor; the latter will only conduct when the signal to the transistor gate is high. In this case, there will be a voltage drop across the load element so that the output is low.

Conversely, when the signal applied to the transistor gate is low, there is no conduction path to ground and hence no voltage drop across the load element, giving high output.

The load element for this type of gate can be a resistor or another transistor. Different types of load elements result in changes in the characteristics of the circuits with respect to such factors as ease of fabrication, packing density and power consumption.

A wide variety of integrated circuits are commercially available for different applications. Some of these comprise just a few logic gates, others have complex circuitry containing many thousands of gates.

4 Microelectronic Memories

4.1 Registers

A computer is made up of a number of different electronic circuits. So far we have considered the logic circuits for such functions as encoding and decoding of information, parity testing, word comparison, addition and subtraction of binary numbers. The equivalent microelectronic circuits may be constructed as described in chapter 3, section 3.7.

These functions are concerned with *decision-making*. A computer additionally needs to be able to *store* information in binary patterns. The main storage of a computer is called the memory.

Computer storage circuits, made from transistors or their microelectronic equivalents, can be built to store binary digits as low or high voltages. Such memory elements are known as *flip-flops* or *latches*. The groups of memory elements are known as *registers* or *memory cells*. Computers contain a number of special-purpose registers as described in the following sections.

Buffer registers

Buffer registers are used within a computer for the temporary storage of information. A buffer register consists of a number of flip-flops, each capable of storing one bit of information, which are controlled by a common signal known as a *clock* (see Figure 4.1).

The state of the flip-flops remains unchanged (latched in their last state) until the clock signal is high. Each flip-flop will then be set when the input signal from the word to be stored is high and reset when it is low.

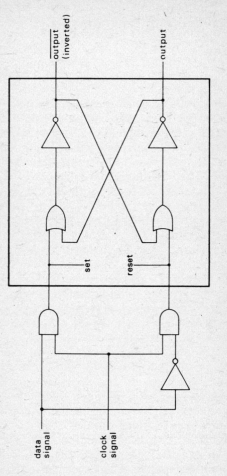

Figure 4.1 A clocked flip-flop

The buffer registers used in modern computers generally have their two-state output converted to three states by three-state switches. The three states are low, high and floating; in the latter case, the output is isolated from the flip-flops. These buffers are known as three-state buffers.

Counters

A counter can be constructed from a number of flip-flops which can perform the functions of reset and carry. The carry is propagated from the least significant flip-flop through to the most significant flip-flop. There is a delay time at each flip-flop; the total propagation delay time increases as the size of the counter is increased (by adding more flip-flops). The worst delay time is the individual delay time multiplied by the number of flip-flops in the counter. These types of counter are known as *ripple* counters.

Synchronous counters clock all the flip-flops at the same time, so that the binary count is achieved after only one propagation delay time whatever the length of the counter. They are therefore much faster than ripple counters but require more complicated circuitry.

A *ring* counter consists of a number of flip-flops built into a circuit which causes the stored bit to move through the flip-flops (starting from the least significant one) and finally back to the first flip-flop. This means that each ring word output from the counter has only one bit set to 1. An 8-bit word ring counter, for example, can be used to activate any one of eight devices according to which of the eight bits is high (has a value of 1).

A computer run consists of a series of operations which are used to process data. One or more digital circuits will be activated to perform these operations, and the timing and sequence of these activities must be accurately controlled. A ring counter may be used to activate the digital circuits at the correct time.

Program counters and accumulators

The use of two other special-purpose registers – program counters and accumulators – are discussed in chapter 5, in the context of their use in computers.

4.2 Computer memories

The memory (main store) of a computer is made up of a large number of registers which are used to hold the instructions (the program) required to solve a particular problem, and some data.

Programs other than the one that is being obeyed may be stored on a backing-store external to the computer memory. In a similar way, the bulk of the data required for a computer run may also be stored on backing-storage. However, data to be operated on by the processing elements of the computer must be in the computer memory during the processing cycle. This is explained further in chapter 5.

There are many different types of memory that have been used in computers. The following sections discuss various microelectronic memories.

Random-access memories (RAMs)

In order to store information, memories need to have circuit elements which can be switched to 0 or 1, and which can retain the patterns of 0s and 1s for the required time.

Figure 4.2 shows a rectangular array of storage cells. Each storage cell consists of an individual circuit as shown in Figure 4.3, and is capable of storing one binary digit as an electric charge on a small capacitor. If the charge is zero then the bit is set to 0; a non-zero charge is used to represent a 1.

Each storage cell in the array has a unique row and column address. This means that a particular storage cell

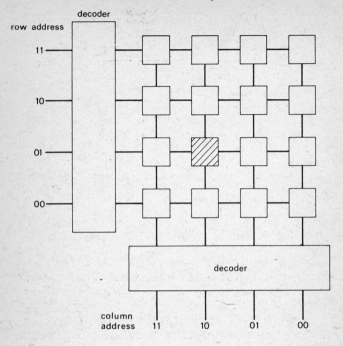

Shaded cell is selected by activating row address 01 and column address 10

Figure 4.2 Memory cell selection

can be selected by the appropriate signals from the row and column address decoders. Although all the transistor switches connected to the activated selection line are turned on, only the *selected* cell will be connected to the data line which is used to transfer one bit of information.

The storage of information is carried out by a 'write' operation. Information is retrieved by a 'read' operation. When information is written into the memory, the read/write input signal causes the required switches to be turned on. However, during the read operation, the

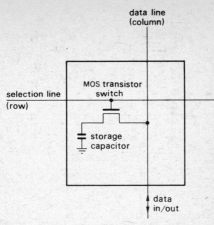

Figure 4.3 Dynamic RAM storage cell

charge on the storage capacitor is reduced since it is shared with the data line capacitance which is much larger. The stored charge is regenerated after each read operation.

Apart from the loss of charge due to the read operation, the stored charge is lost due to the leakage current of the capacitor. This is compensated for by regenerating the charge at regular time intervals related to the time the stored charge takes to leak away, typically a few milliseconds. RAMs which need to be 'refreshed' by regenerated storage charges are known as dynamic RAMs.

Static RAMs use flip-flops for storage and hence do not have to be refreshed. The more complicated circuitry required for each cell results in a larger cell size (for storing one bit of information) compared to a dynamic RAM. Static RAMs also require more power and are more expensive than dynamic RAMs. For example, it may require 40 ma/chip to keep a static RAM in the flip or flop state, whereas an equivalent dynamic RAM may only require 2–4 ma/chip in its quiescent state to maintain its addressing circuitry and input/output interface to the outside world. 40 ma/chip will only be required for the dynamic RAM during its refresh cycle which is about 1½–3% of the total time it is in use. Because of the lower power supply required by the dynamic RAM, smaller cooling systems and cabinets can be used, which makes them suitable for micro- and minicomputers. However, static RAMs have faster access times and hence are used for applications where dynamic RAMs would be too slow. Both types of RAM are volatile, in that the information stored in them disappears when the power is switched off.

The main memories of computers may require a number of single RAM chips as well as driver, error detection and correction circuits. The memory board designer has to take a number of factors into account. In particular, it is essential to design away from the limits of the RAMs. otherwise errors may overlap. It may be necessary to put capacitors across the supply for individual RAMs to ensure a steady voltage for each cycle.

Failure rates for RAM chips can be significant when several of these are linked together to form one memory board. However, it is likely that about 80% of these are single bit failures, that is, only one bit is not stored correctly. Error detection and correction codes are used to enable the computer to continue processing correctly without the user being aware that a hardware fault exists. The maintenance engineer will perform routine tests on information based on error logs and correct the hardware fault (by replacing the faulty chip) when convenient. The Hamming code system is commonly used for error detection and correction.

The Hamming code system

The Hamming code system can be used to detect which data line is at fault and generate the correct bit.

Each group of data lines has a different code generated by parity generators/checkers. The parity (check) bits are stored in a MOS chip. Table 4.1 shows the Hamming numbers associated with four data lines.

| data line | Hamming number | |
	decimal	binary
2^3	4	1 0 0
2^2	3	0 1 1
2^1	2	0 1 0
2^0	1	0 0 1
parity		P4
generator/		P2
checker		P1

Table 4.1 The Hamming code system

Three parity generators/checkers (P4, P2 and P1) are required to generate parity bits for every 4-bit word written into the memory. P4 has input from data line 2^3, P2 from data lines 2^2 and 2^1, and P1 from data lines 2^2 and 2^0.

Suppose a binary word 0101 is to be written into the memory, then the parity bits generated by P4, P2 and P1 will be 101. The signal on line 2^3 is combined with the data bits in its associated Hamming number to give a parity bit of 1. The output from P2 is a combination of the signals on lines 2^2 and 2^1 and their associated Hamming numbers, giving a parity bit of 0. Similarly, the output from P1 is a combination of Hamming numbers 011 and 001, and data bits 1 and 1, giving odd parity i.e. the parity bit is 1.

The parity checkers give a *high* output on checking corresponding to 0 parity bit generation and vice-versa. If the parity bits checked do not correspond to this convention, then the output from the checkers is decoded, and this shows the data line which is at fault. All the bits are checked using a combination of the data bits associated Hamming numbers and the check bits.

Suppose the data word 0101 is read incorrectly as 0001. The output from P4, P2 and P1 will be 011 instead of the expected 010. Decoding 011 gives a Hamming decimal number of 3, that is, the fault is shown to be on the 2^2 line.

The number of check bits (k) plus the number of data lines (n) must be checked. Therefore, k must have a value which results in $2^k - 1 > n + k$. The number of check bits needed becomes proportionally less as the number of data lines increases.

Once the bit which is incorrect has been identified by its Hamming number, circuits are activated to rewrite the word containing the wrong bit; the latter is corrected by inverting it before the data is written back into the RAM. The parity bits are rewritten also into the parity bit store.

This method will only correct single bit failures. 2-bit errors will go undetected, while 3-bit errors will be detected but wrongly corrected.

Read-only memories (ROMs)

Random-access memories are an essential part of a micro-computer, since they are required for the storage of programs during development and for variable data which is input during the running of the program. However, once a program has been developed it can be stored permanently in a read-only memory together with constant data. The program and data can only be accessed when required and cannot be altered.

The binary patterns of information can be built into the chip when it is manufactured. The two binary states can be achieved by having either an open circuit or a connection to ground instead of the storage capacitor in the RAM memory cell previously described. The production of this type of ROM is expensive because of the development cost of designing and laying-out of the circuits and the manufacture of the photomasks for each circuit layer. If many thousands of identical ROMs are required then the development cost can quickly be written off against the relatively cheap fabrication process.

For applications requiring a smaller number of ROMs, it

is possible to purchase programmable read-only memories (PROMs). These are manufactured with a fusible link in each storage cell from the transistor to the ground. The binary patterns can be stored subsequently by blowing the fuses to create open circuits, where required, using appropriate electrical signals. The information stored in the PROM cannot be changed.

During program development, the user may need to change program instructions in a ROM. This may be done by using an erasable programmable ROM (EPROM). A typical EPROM uses an n-channel stacked-gate cell comprising a lower floating gate which stores the cell's charge, and an upper select gate which controls the cell. The select voltage of charged cells is higher than that of uncharged cells, due to the raising of the select voltage threshold when the floating gate is injected with a charge. The charge may be removed by exposing the EPROM to strong ultra-violet light through the small window covering the chip. These devices are known as FAMOS types (Floating-gate Avalanche-injection Metal-Oxide-Semiconductor).

Pin-compatible ROM devices are available which allow the EPROM program to be converted rapidly to a mask-programmed ROM, and the latter can then be plugged into the developed system to replace the EPROM.

All the ROMs described are non-volatile; the information stored as binary patterns is unchanged when the power is switched off, and can be accessed again when power is applied.

Electrically alterable ROMs (EAROMs) are available which are non-volatile, but in addition can be re-programmed during operation. They are too slow and expensive for main computer applications and cannot be used to replace RAM devices in these. However, they are useful for applications which are not time-critical such as point-of-sale terminals and some industrial control systems.

The structure of EAROM devices is similar to the EPROM described previously. The floating gate is replaced by a silicon oxide – silicon nitride interface. The interface is charged or discharged when appropriate electrical signals are applied to the upper aluminium gate. EAROMs based on the FAMOS process have been fabricated as alternatives to the MNOS (Metal-Nitride-Oxide Semi-conductor) device mentioned above. Erasure for these is carried out *in situ* by applying electrical voltages.

Memory addressing

The programmer usually views the computer's memory as a number of locations which can hold data or instructions. Each of these locations must have a unique address so that information can be stored in particular locations and subsequently retrieved from the same memory locations.

We saw in Figure 4.2 how each binary digit contained in an array of storage cells can be uniquely accessed by its row and column address. However, the data and instruction codes required for programming are usually encoded in groups (words) of binary digits. In computers which use a byte (eight bits), as the smallest unit of information which can be accessed, each *byte* in the memory must have a unique address.

The actual memory addresses used for a particular microcomputer will depend on the memory organisation. For example, the RAM memory may consist of more than one RAM chip, in which case the memory address will comprise some bits to select the appropriate chip(s) and some bits to select a particular word within the chip(s) selected. The range of addresses for a memory of $65,536_{10}$ words is

$$0000\ 0000\ 0000\ 0000 \text{ to } 1111\ 1111\ 1111\ 1111$$

However, as far as the programmer is concerned, the address space is 64K (1K = 1024) words which can be accessed uniquely by specifying the addresses within the range given above. Exactly how the address bits and addressable memory are split up is the concern of the logic designer and depends on the architecture (structure) of the computer. A particular architecture may have one or more blocks of memory addresses assigned to RAM, other blocks to ROM, and some blocks for addressing input/output (peripheral) devices; this is explained further in chapter 5.

Memory contents

The patterns of bits contained in words can represent data or program instructions. Data can comprise numerical information in the form of unsigned or signed binary numbers or BCD numbers as discussed in chapter 2. Negative BCD numbers must be preceded by a control word containing 0001; the control word for positive BCD numbers contains 0000.

Data in the form of characters may be encoded in a number of different ways. The 128 symbols defined in the ASCII code (Appendix B) require only seven bits to give a unique representation for each character. The eighth parity bit is used to give even parity.

The part of the computer which is concerned with processing data is called the Central Processing Unit (CPU) or microprocessor in microcomputers. Each type of microprocessor has its own set of instruction codes that it can interpret. The complete set of instructions to carry out a task (the program) is stored in the computer's memory. The instructions are fetched, one at a time, from the memory under the control of the CPU and executed.

Each instruction consists of a number of binary digits which need to be decoded as an instruction code specifying the function or operation to be carried out, and usually an address or operand on which the operation is to be performed. The structure of the CPU and the way it functions is described in chapter 5.

4.3 Serial access memories

Before we leave the subject of microelectronic memories, it is worth looking at two other types of memory known as charge-coupled devices (CCDs) and magnetic-bubble memories.

These are both serial access devices, in which the signal (bit) to be stored is transferred as a charge (CCD device) or magnetised domain (bubble) through the closed loop of the system in a sequential manner, and is not stored until the end of the cycle when it can then be read.

A magnetic bubble memory is made from a chip of garnet material. For information storage, it is necessary to be able to: annihilate bubbles in order to clear the store; generate new bubbles in order to write data; replicate bubbles for non-destructive read-out. Access to the information is provided by propagating bubbles along a defined closed track (major loop) which links write, read and erase stations (see Figure 4.4).

The track along which the bubbles are propagated is defined by patterns of Permalloy deposited on a thin magnetic film grown on to a substrate of gadolinium-gallium-garnate. Bubbles are generated by a current which passes through an electronic circuit in a metallic layer immediately above the magnetic film.

Coils surrounding the chip are used to produce a rotating field which causes the bubbles to be propagated along the major loop. Bubbles are detected when they pass under the Permalloy strips deposited on the bubble-bearing film. The magnetisation of the strips, and hence their resistance, changes due to the presence of a bubble (which represents a 1). The absence of a bubble represents a 0.

Data is transferred from the major loop to minor loops for storage, and is accessed by transferring data from the minor loops after these have been rotated so that the required data is next to the major loop. By using a number of minor loops (for example 157 in one system), the access time can be reduced considerably since one bit from each of the minor loops can be transferred in parallel to the major loop.

One of the main uses of magnetic bubble memories is

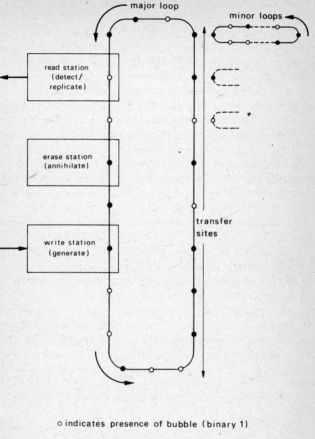

Figure 4.4 schematic element labels:
- major loop
- minor loops
- read station (detect/replicate)
- erase station (annihilate)
- write station (generate)
- transfer sites

○ indicates presence of bubble (binary 1)

● indicates absence of bubble (binary 0)

Figure 4.4 Schematic of magnetic bubble memory

for non-volatile storage in microcomputer systems as an alternative to using magnetic disks (described in chapter 6). Magnetic bubble memories have a number of advantages over disks including non-mechanical access to data, modular structure allowing a low cost/bit for small capacity stores, and simpler interfacing to microprocessors since they can be placed on the same board as the microprocessor.

In CCD memories, each storage cell or segment of the memory loop occupies a smaller area than that required for RAM devices. In addition, simpler circuits are required for signal amplification and refreshing, and address decoding, because of the serial access mode. This means that CCD memories tend to cost less per bit than RAM devices, because fabrication methods are simpler and there is a higher yield. However, serial access is slower than random access, which limits the use of CCD devices to applications where very fast access is not required. CCD devices are particularly useful for analog signal processing such as time delays in the field of telecommunications.

5 Structure and Functions of a Microcomputer

5.1 Basic units

Figure 5.1 shows the structure of a simple microprocessor-based microcomputer. The microprocessor consists of three basic units which perform the following functions:

Synchronisation of processing events and instruction decoding (control unit);
Temporary storage of addresses and data (registers);
Arithmetic, logic and shift operations (arithmetic unit).

Program instructions and data are held in memory (RAM, ROM, PROM, EPROM etc.) until fetched by the control unit signals. Communication to the outside world to various types of peripherals is via one or more input/output ports.

The processing events, controlled by the control unit, are triggered by a quartz crystal clock which generates pulses at regular intervals depending on its frequency. For example, a clock with a frequency of 1 MHz (Megahertz) has a period of 1 μs (microsecond). The clock logic (for driving the clock) may be on the microprocessor chip itself or external to it.

The units are linked by electrical lines which carry electrical pulses representing memory and input/output port addresses (address bus) and data (data bus). A typical 8-bit microprocessor has a 16-line address bus for carrying 2-byte addresses, and an 8-bit data bus for carrying 1-byte data words. Synchronisation signals for controlling the processing events are carried by control lines

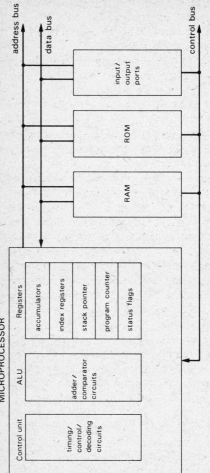

Figure 5.1 Structure of a simple microcomputer

(control bus). The registers, arithmetic and logic unit circuits and memory devices are isolated from the buses by three-state buffers (not shown). Timing and control circuitry is used to ensure that only the device that is transmitting or receiving data is connected to the appropriate bus at any given time.

Microcomputing devices require a small power supply, typically 5v or three levels (+5v, +12v, −5v) depending on the particular devices being used.

At the beginning of a program run, the program counter is set to the address of the first instruction to be executed, subsequently it will be set to the *next* instruction to be executed. The instruction fetch and execution cycles are described in section 5.2.

Status flags are single-bit registers which are set or reset automatically according to the results of arithmetic operations; they can be tested by program instructions. Typical status flags are N, Z and V which record respectively whether the result of an arithmetic operation was negative, zero or was too large to be stored correctly (overflowed). Another flag commonly used is the carry flag (C) which records whether a carry occurred on the left of an addition or subtraction. In each case, the status flag is set to 1 if the specified condition has occurred, otherwise it is set to 0.

Accumulators are registers which are used to store data that has been fetched from memory. Program instructions are available which operate on data held in an accumulator. One or more accumulators are available depending on the particular microprocessor being used.

Index registers are used to hold values which can be used to modify actual memory addresses to produce effective addresses. In this way, the results of previous processing in the program run can be used to alter the sequence in which instructions are obeyed.

Part of the RAM memory of typical microprocessor-based microcomputers is reserved for stack operations. The stack is used, by means of program instructions, to store data temporarily for subsequent retrieval. The data is pushed on to the stack one byte at a time. On retrieval, the top-most byte is pulled off first, that is, the stack operates in LIFO mode (Last-In, First-Out).

The use of accumulators, index registers and stacks is explained later in this chapter.

Chip or bit slice-based microcomputers function in a similar way to microprocessor-based microcomputers. The essential difference is that the computer units may be made up from a number of different chips. For example, the functions of the microprocessor chip can be implemented on several chip slices to overcome the limitations of a particular microprocessor and give improved performance. This philosophy can be extended to the other computer units.

The programming and use of both types of microcomputer is similar. Further detailed discussion will be concerned only with 8-bit microprocessor based microcomputers. 16-bit and 32-bit microprocessors also are available.

5.2   Instruction fetch and execution cycles

The instruction fetch cycle commences with the address of the instruction to be fetched being sent to memory, that is the contents of the program counter is transmitted to the memory.

A read signal is sent to the required memory location by address decoders and causes the contents of this location (the instruction) to be transferred to the instruction register in the control unit. Instruction decoding and control circuits are now activated to operate on the instruction stored in the instruction register. This completes the instruction fetch cycle, during which the program counter is updated to point to the next instruction to be executed.

The microprocessor operations performed during the following cycles depend on the instruction to be executed.

Further accesses to memory may be required to fetch information needed by the instruction. This is followed by an instruction execution cycle which performs storage, arithmetic, logical or shift functions as specified by the instruction or operation code (op code).

The instruction execution cycle is followed by the next instruction fetch cycle, and so on until a halt instruction is obeyed.

5.3 Microprocessor instructions

Each microprocessor 'family' has a fixed set of instructions built into the chip logic. Programs using these binary or equivalent hexadecimal (hex) codes are said to be written in machine code.

Instructions generally consist of two parts, the op code which specifies the operation to be performed, and operands which specify the information to be used in the operation.

The next sections describe the use of accumulators, index registers, stack and memory using examples of typical microprocessor instructions. Mnemonic op codes and decimal operands are used in the examples, since these are easier to understand than binary or hex codes.

Instructions using an accumulator

Data held in memory must be loaded into an accumulator before it can be operated on.

For example, a program to add two numbers together could contain the following sequence of instructions:

Mnemonic op code	Operand (decimal)	Meaning
LDA	5	Load the contents of memory address 5 into the accumulator

Mnemonic op code	Operand (decimal)	Meaning
ADD	25	Add the contents of memory address 25 and put result into accumulator
STA	34	Store the contents of accumulator at memory address 34

The actual op codes will vary according to the particular microprocessor implementation.

Instead of specifying the address of an operand, the instruction can itself contain the actual operand rather than its address. For example:

$$LDA \#5$$

puts the binary representation of 5 (00000101) into the accumulator. The # indicates that the operand is the actual number to be used.

Other instructions of this type in which accumulators and operands are involved include:

Mnemonic	Meaning
SUB	Subtract operand from accumulator contents
AND	AND operand with accumulator
ADC	Add operand plus C flag to accumulator contents

The AND instruction performs the Boolean operation described in chapter 3, section 3.1. The result bit will be 1 if the corresponding bits in the operand and accumulator are *both* 1, otherwise the result bit will be 0. For example, if the accumulator contains 00001011, and the AND operand is 2_{16} (i.e. 00000010), then the number in the accumulator after the instruction has been obeyed is 00000010. The ADC instruction adds in the value of the carry flag (a status flag set to 1 or 0).

Operations not affecting the accumulator

Some instructions operate on the contents of memory locations and leave the accumulator unchanged. For example, DEC, decrements the specified memory location by 1.

Shift instructions are available which operate either on the accumulator or memory contents. For example, ASL (arithmetic shift left) moves the bits in the operand one position to the left. The bit that 'drops off' on the left-hand side of the word is put into the carry register, and the 'gap' on the right is filled by a zero. It is also possible to logically shift to the right (LSR) and rotate to the left or right (ROL and ROR). These instructions allow manipulation of individual bits in a word.

Unconditional and conditional branching

Most problems require a decision to be made at different stages in the program, so that alternative logical paths can be followed according to the result of a test. It is possible to test the status flags and to jump backwards or forwards to a different instruction in the program by offsetting the contents of the program counter by the specified amount if the test is true.

Instructions using index registers

As was mentioned in section 5.1, index registers can be used to produce effective addresses. Op codes are available which indicate that the operation is indexed. For example,

> LDAX 300
> will load the contents of the memory address
> 300 + the contents of index register X

that is, if index register X contains 6 then the contents of memory address 306 will be loaded. If this instruction is encountered again during the program run, and this time index register X contains 8, then the contents of 308 will be loaded. Instructions are available for changing the contents of index registers. For example, DEX and INX, can be used as mnemonics for op codes which subtract 1 from or add 1 to index register X. This gives the programmer a means of handling lists and tables, since different memory addresses can be accessed using the same set of indexed instructions. The effective memory address at any given point during the program run depends on the contents of the index register at that stage.

Subroutines and stack operations

Sequences of instructions that are used more than once, either in the same program or in a different program, may be used in the form of subroutines. Each subroutine (particular sequence of instructions) needs to be written only once, thus saving program development time. Additionally, if the subroutine is used more than once in a program, only one set of the subroutine instructions needs to be entered into the computer with a resultant saving in storage space.

Program control is transferred to the subroutine during execution by means of a Jump to Subroutine instruction (JSR). The effect of this instruction is to put the return address on to the stack, and the address of the first instruction in the subroutine into the program counter so that execution can continue from this new address.

At the end of the execution of the subroutine instructions, program control had to be returned to the instruction *following* the one that called the subroutine. This is achieved by the RTS (Return from Subroutine) instruction, which is the last instruction in each subroutine. When this instruction is executed, the return address is retrieved from the stack and placed in the program counter, which is then incremented so that it points to the instruction following the JSR instruction.

The contents of the stack pointer register is changed whenever a stack operation is carried out, so that it points to the *latest* information that is on the stack.

Instructions are available to the programmer for pushing information on to the stack or pulling information off, but their use is outside the scope of this book.

The use of some of the machine code instructions mentioned in this chapter is illustrated in the programming examples given in chapter 6, section 6.2 and chapter 7, section 7.2.

5.4   Peripheral equipment

The microcomputer has to communicate with the outside world, so that programs and data can be entered into its memory and processed information can be displayed or transmitted in some form to the microcomputer user.

There are various types of peripheral equipment that may be attached to microcomputers including keyboards and paper tape readers for input, and visual display units (vDUs) and printers for output. Information may be output from the microcomputer on to magnetic tape or disk for storage and re-entered when required.

Different sensors and actuators may be linked (interfaced) to the microcomputer for controlling instruments and machines; their use is discussed in later chapters.

Keyboards

A keyboard consists of a number of switches which are activated by pressure or simply by touching them. The keys are arranged as a matrix, so that the depression of any key can be detected by scanning the rows and columns of the matrix. Hardware may be used to sense which key has been pressed or this may be carried out by a software routine.

The layout of the keyboard may be similar to that of the conventional typewriter or may be designed for particular users. For example, if a large amount of the data to be entered is generally numeric, then a numeric key pad containing keys for decimal 0 through 9, full stop, and some special characters, is an essential feature.

Teletypewriters

Teletypewriters may be used for a number of different purposes in computer systems. For example, they may be used as terminals to transmit and receive information over telephone lines or as input/output devices directly connected to a computer.

Teletypewriters transmit and receive information in serial form, that is, each character is converted to a bit-code, (e.g. ASCII) and then sent as a stream of serial data bits with start and stop control bits for each character. The characters have to be decoded when they reach the computer end.

Because the microprocessor is operating at a much higher speed than the peripherals, and often has to receive and transmit information from and to a number of peripherals all trying to communicate at the same time, all information transfer is carried out via buffers. The buffers store information temporarily until the microcomputer is ready to receive or transmit it.

Teletypewriters and other terminals using telephone lines require modems (modulators-demodulators) at each end, to convert the data to a form suitable for voice transmission and vice-versa.

As well as having a keyboard, teletypewriters are fitted with a printing device, so that a hard copy of the information sent and received is available. Characters are printed one at a time by movement of the block, containing the characters, across the paper from left to right. The selected character is pressed against a typewriter ribbon to give a solid shape. Speeds vary from about 10–30 characters/second.

Teletypewriters may have paper tape stations for producing output on to punched paper tape. Characters are encoded, usually in seven positions, across the paper tape with an eighth position to give even parity. A sprocket hole between the third and fourth positions is used to feed the paper tape. The paper tape is read by pins protruding through the punched holes as it is fed through the reading station. Some paper tape readers have circuity to detect whether a parity error has occurred, that is, if an odd number of holes is present in any one row (frame) on the paper tape. This error detection device reduces the number of wrong characters that are transmitted.

Visual display units

These units have a cathode-ray tube (CRT) for displaying information and often a keyboard which may be attached or is detachable. The VDU may be part of a self-contained microcomputer, with all the necessary circuitry contained in the case holding the CRT.

The output from the keyboard is decoded into a form suitable for the computer being used. This function is usually carried out within the VDU which may also have its own buffer, so that information keyed in is not transmitted immediately giving the operator a chance to correct it.

Other more sophisticated features may be available on more expensive VDUs such as graphics facilities and screen-editing. With the latter facility, changes may be made to information displayed on the screen by moving a special character (cursor) to the position on the screen which requires alteration. Often these facilities will be under the control of programs stored in ROMs on the VDU board. Additionally, a light pen may be used as an input device by pointing it to the required position on the screen.

Other printers

A common type of inexpensive printer available for use with microcomputers has a head containing a matrix of pins. The pins which form particular characters are selected by a decoder. This sends pulses to operate solenoids controlling the pin movement. The type and density of the characters depends on the number of pins in the matrix and on programmed control via a ROM. Some matrix printers allow the shape and size of the character to be programmed.

Printing may be unidirectional or bidirectional at speeds from about 100 characters/second upwards. Printers may use friction feed or traction feed (sprocket feed) for paper movement. Some printers have attachments for both facilities including variable width tractors and devices for feeding single sheets of stationery, such as headed notepaper.

A more expensive printer, which is suitable for word-processing applications, where good quality printing is required, uses a rotating daisy wheel for printing solid characters. Different sets of characters may be used simply by changing the daisy wheel, which contains the characters along its perimeter. Many sophisticated features are available under ROM program control, including carriage and print head movement control.

Magnetic recording devices

There are basically two types of devices, serial access, e.g. magnetic tape, and random access, e.g. magnetic disk.

Information is recorded magnetically on both these media, which generally consist of a substrate made from a plastics material coated with magnetic oxide. A 1 bit is represented by a portion of magnetised material (magnetic spot) and a 0 bit by the absence of a magnetic spot. Patterns of 1s and 0s are used to represent character codes (e.g. ASCII).

Ordinary portable cassette recorders and standard audio cassettes can be used with some microcomputers. Standard cassette interfaces are used to allow binary information in the microcomputer memory to be transmitted as a serial bit stream for recording on tape. The 1 and 0 bits are generated as two different tones.

Check characters are written at the end of each block of data to give a horizontal parity check, as well as the vertical parity checks for each character. Each block has a header by which it can be identified. Trailer bytes indicate the end of each block. Read and write heads detect or record the magnetic patterns. Erasure of information is effected by over-writing the old data with new data. Reel-to-reel magnetic tape units work in a similar way.

Magnetic disks have data recorded on them in a series of circular tracks. Each track is divided into sectors and is uniquely identified. Data is transferred in sectors or groups of these. Read/write heads are moved to the appropriate track for recording or accessing data under hardware/software control, so that random access of data can be achieved. Indexes may be used to enable the required data to be located or data may be retrieved randomly by using relative addressing, in which data is recorded in known positions. Data may also be recorded serially as on magnetic tape.

Two types of disk are commonly used, floppy (flexible) disks and hard disks. Floppy disks are available in two sizes, standard 8 inches and mini 5¼ inches. Hard or soft sectoring may be employed. The former uses holes to identify the sectors, whereas the latter uses magnetic recording for sector identification. Extra information may be stored by increasing the density of recording; double density disks can have twice as much data packed into each track. In addition, two heads or a double-sided head can be used to access both surfaces of the disk. Disk units often have dual drives attached to one controller.

The microcomputer user usually requires no knowledge of the hardware implementation of the disk system. The floppy disk controller contains a disk-operating system for carrying out various functions such as allocating space and names to data files, formatting information on the disk, random and sequential accessing, input/ouput buffering, file editing including renaming and deletion of files, disk space re-organisation, error detection and output of diagnostic messages to indicate the cause of errors. This software is often contained in a ROM but may require some of the user RAM store in the microcomputer for its operation. Standard disk operating systems are available to allow transportability of disk-based software between microcomputer systems which use the appropriate standard.

Hard disk drives, available for use with microcomputers, are usually based on Winchester technology. The units consist of a hard disk totally enclosed and sealed in a chamber. This ensures that extraneous particles of dust or dirt cannot get into the very small gap between the fast spinning disk and the floating read/write head, as this would cause a head-crash which would ruin the head and disk resulting in the loss of all the information held on the disk. The disks are the same size (8 inches diameter) as standard floppy disks, but can hold much more data and have greater reliability.

Winchester technology systems are much cheaper than the standard 14 inch hard disk systems used with larger computers. Their main drawback is that they are not removable, and require tape back-up for storage of information, so that the disk can be used for many different files. Some Winchester systems incorporate cartridge back-up.

6 Communication with Peripheral Devices

6.1 Input/output considerations

Peripheral equipment may be of the type discussed in chapter 5. Additionally, sensors, actuators and display devices may be attached to the microcomputer for measuring, monitoring and control applications in industry, in laboratories or in the home.

The data enters or leaves the microcomputer via its input/output ports. The type of port required depends on the nature of the data that the peripheral device can output or receive. The microcomputer handles data in parallel form, for example, 1 byte (8 bits) at a time. Some peripheral devices send and receive streams of single bits, which have to be converted to parallel form and vice-versa. This can be accomplished by hardware or software methods.

Communication is carried out over address, data and control lines (buses). The function of each line needs to be the same across the interface between the microcomputer and the peripheral device. Several standard parallel and bit-serial buses have been specified, so that peripheral equipment with standard interfaces can be plugged directly into compatible microcomputer input/output ports. If the peripheral device has a different interface, then another interface which performs the necessary conversion needs to be inserted between the peripheral and the microcomputer.

As well as matching the interfaces, the transfer of data has to be controlled. The peripheral and microcomputer need to pass information to each other, indicating when they are ready to transmit. In addition, the timing of the transfers has to be synchronised, as the microcomputer and peripherals are likely to be operating at different speeds and more than one peripheral may need to communicate with the microcomputer at any one time.

These problems are discussed in the following sections.

6.2   Programmable parallel input/output ports

The parallel input/output port (PIO) available on most microcomputers is likely to be programmable. Common types of PIO have two 8-bit ports, giving 16 bi-directional input/output lines. All the circuits to perform the PIO operations are on one chip which is mounted in a conventional 40-pin DIP. Each pin is used to transmit or receive an electrical signal.

All communication between the microprocessor and the PIO takes place over a data bus (8 pins). 16 pins connect the two input/output ports with the external logic of peripheral devices. Although each of these lines can be designated for input or output, a single pin cannot transmit data in both directions. Other pins are used for selecting devices and associated memory addresses, and for control and timing.

Each of the two input/output ports has a data direction register, a data buffer and a control register. The data buffer is used for holding input or output information temporarily, before it is transferred to the microprocessor or to the device. Each bit of the data direction registers has to be set to 0 or 1 to designate the associated pins of the input/output ports as input or output respectively. The control registers are used to define the mode of operation of the I/O ports and to record the status of interrupt requests.

A device may send a signal to the microcomputer to interrupt the current processing, so that the processing requirements of the device may be carried out. This allows devices which have high priority, such as those used in process control applications, to be serviced without appreciable delay. The microprocessor has to complete the instruction it is processing and save the current status of the program, before servicing the interrupt, so that afterwards it can resume processing where it left off. This method is explained in more detail in section 6.4.

The following example illustrates typical programming instructions that may be used to control a device using a PIO.

Using a PIO

```
      Instruction                          Comments

      LDA# FO                ]             set output
      STA  ODRA                            definition
      LDA# 09                              registers
      STA  ODRB              ]

ENTER LDX# 21                ]             put hex code from keyboard (see also Table 7.1)
      JSR  ('fetch data' subroutine) ]    into address 21
      LDA  PORTB
      ORA# 08                              switch on
      AND# 08                              'ready' light
      STA  PORTB            ]

AGAIN LDA  PORTA             ]             loop until push-button
      BNE  AGAIN                           switches are open

WAIT  LDA  PORTA             ]             loop until at least one
      BEQ  WAIT                            switch has been processed

      LDX# FF                ]
LOOP1 LDY# FF
LOOP2 DEY                                  time delay to allow all
      BNE  LOOP2                           selected push-button
      DEX                                  switches to be closed
      BNE  LOOP1            ]

      LDA  PORTA             ]             test correct
      CMPZ 21                              combination
      BNE  AGAIN                           of switches

      LDA  PORTB             ]             switch on
      ORA# 01                              PB0 light
      AND# 01
      STA  PORTB            ]

      JMP  ENTER                           return to enter
```

Table 6.1 Program using a PIO

The objective of the program shown in Table 6.1 is to enter a hex code from the microcomputer's keyboard and then switch on a ready light. Another user tries to guess the binary pattern represented by the hex code by pressing 1 to 4 push-button switches. If the correct pattern is chosen, the ready light is switched off and another light comes on. Otherwise another guess can be tried.

The instruction mnemonics shown in Table 6.1 are those for a typical 8-bit microprocessor (the MOS Technology MCS 6502) used in many microcomputers such as the Acorn, ACT, Aim, Apple, BBC, Challenger, Commodore PET, VIC and KIM, Microtan, Superboard, SYM and UK 101.

This microprocessor addresses the input/output ports as though they were memory locations. Similar instructions are used with the Motorola 6800 microprocessor. Microprocessors such as the Intel 8080/85 and Zilog Z80 use special input/output instructions.

PIOs which may be used in a similar way to that shown in the example, include the MOS Technology MCS 6522, the Motorola MC 6820 and the National Semi-conductor INS 8154. Each of these PIOs has two 8-bit input/output ports giving sixteen lines which may be designated as input or output by setting bit positions in two registers, called data direction registers (DDR) or output definition registers (ODR).

A 0 or a 1 in a particular bit position in ODRA and ODRB assigns the corresponding pin in the associated ports as input or output respectively. In the example ODRA is set to $F0_{16}$, that is 11110000_2, which designates the eight lines in port A as follows:

PA7 to PA4 output, PA3 to PA0 input.

PA0 to PA3 are attached to four push-button switches as shown in Figure 6.1. PA4 to PA7 are not used in the example.

ODRB is set to 09_{16}, that is 00001001_2, which designates PB3 and PB0 in port B as output; the remaining pins are

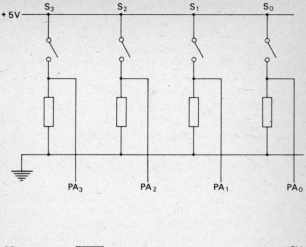

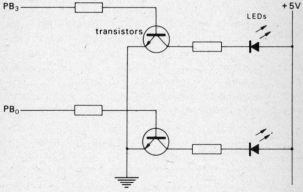

Figure 6.1 Switch and LED circuits

assigned as input but are not used in the example. PB0 and PB3 are attached to LEDs as shown in Figure 6.1.

After the initialisation instructions for the output definition registers, the program starts at ENTER by accepting a 2-digit hexadecimal code (01 to 0F) from the keyboard by means of a subroutine (not shown). This code is stored as a binary pattern at address 21.

The OR instruction puts a 1 in the accumulator in every position where there is a 1 in *either* or *both* the accumulator and the OR operand. Since $08_{16} = 00001000_2$, bit 3 in the accumulator is set to 1 by ORA# 08.

The AND instruction puts a 1 in the accumulator in every position where there is a 1 in *both* the accumulator and the AND operand. AND# 08 results in a 1 being placed in the accumulator *only* in bit 3.

When the contents of the accumulator is stored in PORTB, a high voltage (about 5v) is put on PB3 only, so that the LED attached to PB3 (the ready light) is switched on, and the LED on PB0 is switched off.

The program loops around AGAIN until no push-button switches are down, and then waits for a switch to be pressed. Two further loops (LOOP 1 and LOOP 2) give a short time delay, depending on the number of machine cycles required for the execution of each instruction and the frequency of the clock. This allows time for a combination of switches to be pressed. Each switch that is pressed puts a high voltage on one of the lines PA0, PA1, PA2 or PA3, so that a binary pattern of four bits is formed.

This binary pattern in PORTA is compared with that stored at address 21 (previously input at ENTER) using the CMPZ instruction. If the patterns are not the same, the program jumps back to AGAIN so that a different combination of push-button switches can be pressed.

When the correct combination of switches has been pressed, the LED attached to PB0 is switched on and that on PB3 is switched off, using ORA# 01 and AND# 01 to put a high voltage on PB0 only as shown.

Finally, the program returns to ENTER so that another 2-digit hexadecimal code can be entered.

6.3 Serial input/output

Integrated circuits are available which convert streams of serial bits to parallel form and vice-versa. Such devices are generally classified as Universal Asynchronous Receiver-Transmitters (UARTs). Special UARTs are available for use with microprocessor based systems.

The ICs may handle either synchronous or asynchronous serial input/output protocols or both types of protocol. Single chips which handle the latter are known as Universal Synchronous-Asynchronous Receiver-Transmitters (USARTs).

When synchronous protocol is used to transfer serial data, a data bit is sent over the communications line at regular time intervals. The transmission rate is often quoted in bauds (the number of bits/second). For example, a baud rate of 110 indicates that 110 data bits are sent every second. Baud rates can vary from 110–9600. The start of each character transmitted is indicated by one or two synch characters. The transmitting device may not be ready to send characters continuously; synch characters are sent when no actual characters are being transmitted.

When the alternative mode for transmitting serial data is used, asynchronous protocol, the transmitting device only sends a character if one is ready to be sent. The start and end of characters is indicated by a start and one or two stop bits.

A typical USART has an 8-bit bi-directional data bus, which is used for transferring a byte of parallel data or a control code from the microprocessor to the USART. The control code indicates in which mode the USART is to be used, synchronous or asynchronous. The data bus is also used to transfer data, or the contents of a status register, from the USART to the microprocessor. The latter can access the USART either by given memory addresses or as input/output ports. Therefore input/output operations are carried out when the microprocessor executes either a memory reference instruction or an input/output instruction. The data is transferred via buffers in the USART, which are used also for the assembly of serial-bit data into 8-bit parallel data and for converting parallel data into the serial data stream required for the particular protocol being used.

The status register bits can be tested, so that different sequences of instructions are executed depending on conditions recorded in the register.

The correct transmission of data according to the protocol selected is carried out by the USART under program control.

6.4　Data transfer methods

Data is transferred between the microcomputer and peripheral devices using three different types of method. Two of these have been briefly mentioned previously, namely, programmed input/output methods where the transfer is controlled by the program being executed in the microprocessor, and interrupt input/output methods in which the microprocessor program is interrupted by requests from the devices when they need the attention of the microprocessor. A third type of method does not involve the microprocessor for the transfer process; the transfer takes place between the memory and the peripheral and is called Direct Memory Access (DMA).

An outline of these methods follows. Some applications may require a combination of these methods for different devices.

Programmed input/output

Programmed input/output is also known as polling, because the microcomputer program controlling the transfers continually checks or polls the status of each peripheral device in turn to see if data needs to be transferred to or from the device.

The status of the devices is indicated by 1-bit flags stored in the controller chips interfacing the devices to the microcomputer. The transfer is carried out under the control of signals from the microprocessor. The speed of the latter is matched to the speed of the slow peripheral device, for example a teletype sending and receiving data at 110 bauds, by using buffers in the peripheral's controller. This means that the microprocessor can carry on processing until an input buffer is full and is ready to be transferred to the microcomputer, or until an output buffer is empty and can be filled with data to be transmitted to the peripheral device.

The microcomputer program controls the transfers by either special input/output instructions or by instructions which address an input/output port, depending on the microprocessor. The routine for outputting a character to a device controller buffer needs to check that the buffer is empty, that is, the device is ready to receive more data. Typically, the peripheral status flag is loaded into an accumulator and tested to see if the flag is set for ready; if it is, the character is output to the buffer in the controller. If the flag is set to busy (not ready) then the program routine loops back to perform the sequence of instructions again.

Similarly, the input routine tests the peripheral status flag to check whether the input buffer is full and the character contained in the buffer can be loaded. Figure 6.2 shows flow-charts for the two routines.

Interrupt input/output

Programmed input/output may be too slow for peripheral devices that need a fast response from the microcomputer, such as sensors, actuators and display devices used in process control applications.

An interrupt signal is sent from the device or its controller to the microprocessor whenever the device requires servicing. For example, a sensing device may send a value (temperature, pressure, etc.) to the microcomputer for comparison with a set value or range of values, and the microcomputer may be programmed to send a control signal to open or close a valve to regulate the condition of the environment being measured.

The presence of an interrupt is checked by the micro-

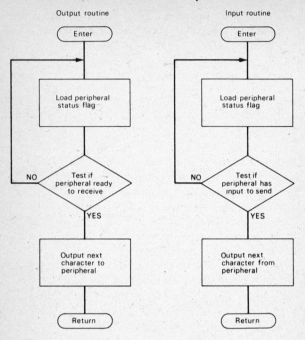

Figure 6.2   Polling routines

computer after the processing of each instruction. The microprocessor will enable (accept) the interrupt only if one of the microprocessor's flags, the interrupt mask, is set to 0. The interrupt mask is set to 1 when the interrupt has been acknowledged by the microprocessor, so that no other interrupt can be accepted until the current one has been serviced. An exception to this is a non-maskable interrupt (NMI) which cannot be disabled and can interrupt any routine; this is used for servicing termination conditions such as powerdown.

Next the microprocessor pushes the contents of the program counter, index register(s), accumulator(s) and status register on to the stack. Some microprocessors do this automatically, others only store the program counter by hardware and the contents of the remaining registers is stored by the interrupt service routine (software). The saving of the status of the program is essential to enable the microprocessor to continue processing from where it was suspended by the interrupt service routine.

More than one device may be attached to the same interrupt line. The microprocessor has to identify which device sent the request, so that the address of the start of the appropriate service routine can be loaded into the program counter. This may be done by software which checks the interrupt bit in the status registers of each device to determine the devices requiring attention and their priority.

This software method may be too slow for some applications, which may require the faster response provided by an interrupt vectoring method based on external hardware. Priority-Interrupt Controller (PIC) integrated circuits are available, which supply the address of the appropriate interrupt service routine when requesting an interrupt. In addition, PICs have facilities for determining interrupt priorities associated with particular pins. A priority level can be set by the programmer; this level is compared, inside the PIC, with those of interrupts requiring service. An interrupt is inhibited if its level is lower than that set in the PIC.

Direct Memory Access

Direct Memory Access (DMA) methods use hardware to service devices such as disks and some graphics display units, which have a high transfer rate.

The hardware device used to process the transfer is known as a Direct Memory Access Controller (DMAC). As with most logic chips, the design and capabilities of these processors varies from manufacturer to manufacturer. DMAC devices are available which have been designed so that they may be used with most microcomputer systems.

Since the function of the DMAC is to transfer data at high speed between the peripheral device and memory, it will need to use the address and data buses. A typical microprocessor has a HOLD or HALT state during which the address and data buses and the read/write control is floated, that is, the microprocessor disconnects itself from the system buses. During this time the microprocessor cannot carry out any processing.

Note: HOLD and HALT have the *same* function in some microprocessors, whereas other microprocessors have both HALT and HOLD states which have *different* functions. We will use HOLD for indicating the state during which the system buses are floated.

The sequence of operations is as follows:

Device sends an interrupt request to DMAC;
DMAC sends HOLD signal to microprocessor;
Microprocessor completes execution of current instruction;
It then acknowledges the HOLD signal and suspends itself by floating the system buses;
DMAC places the memory address associated with the data transfer on the address bus (the source and destination of the data is held in registers within the DMAC, which are under program control);
DMAC generates control signals for read or write, thus causing data to be sent along the data bus from the peripheral device to the memory or vice versa;
On completion of the transfer, bus control is returned to the microprocessor so that it can resume processing.

The DMAC is able to perform these operations because it contains similar logic to the microprocessor, including address and status registers and a counter indicating the length of the data block to be transferred from the appropriate buffer.

A DMAC may have the capability of operating in more than one mode. The data may be transferred one byte at a time (single byte mode) or the DMAC may continue to transfer data if there is some ready to be processed (burst mode). In these cases, bus control is returned to the microprocessor after the transfer of one byte or if no data is ready to be transferred, respectively. Continuous mode may also be available, in which the DMAC does not relinquish bus control until the DMA operation has been entirely completed.

These three modes cause a slowing down of the program execution, whereas the fourth mode of operation does not. This mode is called cycle stealing or transparent mode, since the DMA transfers occur during part of the instruction fetch machine cycles so that the program is unaware of their occurrence.

A sophisticated type of DMAC is capable of more than the transfer of a block of data. Facilities are provided for the DMAC to identify a byte which matches the pattern set in a match register. A block of data may be searched for a matching byte or a matching byte may be detected during the transfer of a block of data. This allows, for example, the transmission of data to be terminated when a matching byte is encountered. Any one of the operating modes may be used for each type of processing.

6.5 Bus and interface standards

Communication lines which link modules and systems must be matched. Several standard buses have been specified for both parallel and bit-serial operations.

Parallel buses

One standard commonly used is the s100 bus. As its name implies, it has 100 lines, each of which is capable of being used for a particular purpose. Lines are dedicated to the transfer of data uni-directionally (that is, there are separate input and output lines), addresses, interrupts, control functions and power supplies.

Many manufacturers supply s100 boards or systems; not all of these are compatible because of different implementations of some of the lines. However, the popularity of the s100 bus gives the system builder a wide choice of modules for constructing general – or special – purpose microcomputer systems.

A parallel bus used for connecting systems, for example printers and measuring equipment to microcomputers, is based on a standard (IEEE-488) specified by the Institute of Electrical and Electronic Engineers. This bus has sixteen lines for carrying signals divided up into three groups called the data bus, the management bus and the transfer bus.

The IEEE-488 *data bus* comprises eight bidirectional lines for transferring addresses, data and device commands (control information) between the microcomputer and external devices. Five further communication lines (the management bus) are used for system control.

Since the data lines carry data or commands, one of the system control lines needs to indicate which type of information is being transmitted. When a device requires servicing, another control line will send a signal to the microcomputer. A third control line signals the microcomputer when data transfer is complete. The remaining two general control lines are concerned with setting devices for local or remote operation, and for setting the system to a known state.

Transfer of data between the microcomputer and the devices linked to it via the IEEE-488 interface is performed over three further control lines (the transfer bus). These allow signals to be sent from the sender and acceptor of data. One control line indicates whether the data on the data lines is valid or not. The two other control lines indicate whether the acceptor (listening device) is ready or not to accept data from the source (talker), and whether it has been accepted or not.

Devices are allocated a number by the microcomputer system. One microcomputer, for example, allocates numbers 0, 1, 2, 3 for its keyboard, two cassette recorders and video screen. Devices connected to the microcomputer's IEEE-488 port are allocated numbers 4 through 30. Device numbers are set in the devices themselves by hardware switching.

The IEEE-488 bus can be implemented using secondary as well as primary addresses. This means that a peripheral device can function in a number of different modes under software control. For example, a printer can be used to print in different formats according to commands set in the program using it.

Serial buses

A common standard for the transmission of data in serial form (RS232C) has been specified by the Electronics Industry Association (EIA). Although 25 lines are specified by this standard, not all of these are necessarily implemented by manufacture of equipment using RS232C interfaces. 25-pin D-type connectors are usually used to connect devices.

Lines are available for sending and receiving data, requesting data and indicating that it may be sent, indicating readiness to receive and accept data, and selecting the data rate.

Most terminals, including teletypewriters, VDUs and printers, have RS232C interfaces for communicating either directly with computers or over telephone and special data lines using modems.

These RS232C devices may be linked to a microcomputer's IEEE-488 port by using an IEEE-488/RS232C interface to convert the signals. Only some of the signals need to be converted if data is to be transmitted in one direction only, for example, from the microcomputer to a printer. An RS232C peripheral device, which is used for input and output, would require a bidirectional IEEE-488/RS232C interface. A similar situation arises when there is a requirement to link a laboratory instrument, that has an

IEEE-488 interface, to a microcomputer's asynchronous serial input/output port.

A general-purpose interface of this kind would usually be designated to operate at different baud rates, so that it can be made compatible with a number of different devices, by setting switches. Such interfaces are available commercially and are supplied with operating instructions including switch settings.

6.6   Analog and digital conversion methods

The peripheral devices we have considered so far transmit and receive digital (discrete high or low) signals. Many measuring and control devices operate with analog signals, which are changing continuously rather than in discrete steps. This means that the signals transmitted to the microcomputer for processing must be converted from analog to digital (A/D) form, and digital control signals sent from the microcomputer to the peripheral device have to be converted to analog form (D/A) before they reach the device.

A/D and D/A converters are available as integrated circuits. A typical D/A converter has circuits which generate a current corresponding to each bit-position of the binary number to be converted. For example, a converter for an 8-bit binary number outputs a current in the proportions 1:2:4:8:16:32:64:128, according to which bit-position is set, and sums all the currents.

The binary number 00001010 would be converted to a current which is ten times as large as that output for 00000001. The total current can be converted to a voltage using an operational amplifier built into the D/A converter.

D/A converter ICs are specified as having a certain resolution and speed. The resolution specifies the accuracy of the conversion. For example, 8-bit converters have an accuracy of approximately 1 part in 250, whereas 16-bit converters give an accuracy better than 1 part in 65,000

A/D converters use one of three different techniques to perform the conversion. The most suitable IC to use for a particular application depends on the speed and accuracy required.

In each case, the analog signal has to be sampled at a rate which gives sufficient values (samples) during a particular time period, so that the digital representation of these values accurately reflects the analog signal over this time period.

Successive-approximation method

The successive-approximation conversion method uses a comparator which has inputs from the analog signal being converted and from a D/A converter output. The latter outputs a 1 bit from the most significant (left-most) bit-position, and only resets this to 0 if the comparator output is 0. The comparison continues with the next least significant bit in the binary word until each bit has been compared and set according to the comparator output. The final settings in the binary word is the digital representation of the analog signal.

Analog integration method

Analog integration is a conversion method which is more accurate than the successive-approximation method, although slower. The unknown positive voltage of the analog signal to be converted is used to charge a capacitor for a fixed period of time. The value of this voltage is found by integrating it with a negative reference voltage, whose value is known. The effect of this is to cause the capacitor to be discharged in a certain time; a measurement of this time together with the fixed time and voltage parameters is used to determine the value of the unknown voltage to be represented digitally.

Direct comparison method

The third method requires a number of comparators and reference voltages to allow a direct comparison to be made. 2^n-1 comparators are required, so that a 4-bit converter requires fifteen comparators; this together with the complex circuitry needed makes such devices expensive, although very fast compared to the other two methods.

Interfacing converters

A detailed discussion of the techniques used for interfacing D/A and A/D converters to microcomputers is outside the scope of this book. Basically, D/A converters are interfaced to output ports; some D/A converters contain a buffer for holding the word which the D/A is converting. A/D converters are interfaced to input ports and are polled or interrupt techniques are used.

7 Programming a Microcomputer

7.1 Machine level programming

The only language that the computer understands is its own machine code (binary code). Programs written in machine code need to be assembled by specifying the memory location of each byte of all the instructions in their correct sequence.

The programming task is simplified by using mnemonic op codes and operands to express the logic of the program. The program can be hand assembled from its mnemonic form in the following way.

First, each instruction is given the correct memory address in which its op code will be stored. Most of the instructions will be more than one byte long, so the actual length of each instruction must be taken into account. The complete set of instructions in the program are listed as hex op codes and hex addresses. Mnemonic labels are listed in a symbol table and converted to actual addresses, that is, the addresses of the first bytes of the instructions which are labelled. This table is used for reference purposes when an actual address needs to be inserted into a JMP or JSR instruction.

When the program has been assembled, it can be keyed into the microcomputer as explained in section 7.3.

7.2 Machine code program example

Table 7.1 shows the logic and coding of a simple machine code program. The program takes two 2-digit hex numbers from the keyboard and displays the larger one. If the numbers are equal, then two further numbers are keyed in.

| page/byte | machine code (hex) | | | flowchart | mnemonic code | | |
	1st byte	2nd byte	3rd byte		label	op code	operands
0300	F8			start		SED	
0301	A2	21				LDX#	21
0303	20	88	FE	fetch		JSR	('fetch data')
0306	38			N1,N2		SEC	
0307	A5	21		A←N1	REPEAT	LDAZ	N1
0309	E5	22		A←N1−N2		SBC	N2
030B	F0	F6		A=0? yes		BEQ	REPEAT
030D	90	05		A<1? yes		BCC	LOADN2
030F	A5	21		A←N1		LDAZ	N1
0311	4C	16	03	A←N2 LOADN2 display A DISPLAY		JMP	DISPLAY
0314	A5	22				LDAZ	N2
0316	20	60	FE			JSR	('display')
0319	4C	04	FF	restart		JMP	(restart)

Table 7.1 Display the larger of two numbers

The instructions are shown in both machine code (hexadecimal) and mnemonic form for the MOS Technology 6502 8-bit microprocessor. However, the program can be readily converted to other microprocessor codes.

The 6502 microprocessor can address 2^{16} (65,536) bytes of memory. This memory is divided up into smaller storage areas called pages, each of which contains 256 bytes. The pages are numbered from 00_{16} to FF_{16}. The program given in Table 7.1 has the start byte of the first instruction stored at memory address 0300_{16}, that is, in page 03, byte 00.

Page 00 is known as *zero page*. There are special op codes for instructions referring to addresses in zero page. These instructions only require the particular byte within zero page to be specified for memory references. This means that zero page instructions are one byte shorter than the equivalent instructions which refer to memory addresses in other pages, since for these one extra byte is needed to specify the page number.

The two numbers (N1 and N2) to be compared are stored in zero page in bytes 21 and 22. Therefore LDAZ instructions (two bytes long) may be used to load these numbers into the accumulator, rather than the LDA instruction which uses *absolute* addresses and is three bytes long.

It is assumed that the microcomputer to be used has a monitor program in ROM which has a number of different subroutines to allow operations such as:

Entry of data and instructions in hexadecimal code from the keyboard or from cassette;
Storage of programs on cassette tapes;
Fetching of numbers from the keboard so that data may be keyed in during execution of the program;
Display of hex digits on an LED display.

The program starts with the instruction SED (set decimal mode), so that calculations will be carried out in binary coded decimal (BCD). The addresses where the numbers are to be stored (in bytes 21 and 22 in zero page) are indicated to the 'fetch data' subroutine which has RTS as its last instruction. When the RTS instruction has been obeyed control is returned to the main routine and the SEC instruction, which sets the carry flag, is executed next.

The carry flag is tested after N2 has been subtracted from N1 which is in the accumulator, using SBC (subtract with carry). If N1 and N2 are equal, then the result of the test BEQ (branch if equal) is true and the program will branch back to the label REPEAT, that is, ten bytes back $(F6_{16} = -10_{10})$. Two more 2-digit numbers can then be entered from the keyboard. If the two numbers are not equal, the next instruction that is executed is BCC (branch if carry clear). The carry flag is cleared after the SBC instruction has been obeyed if the contents of the accumulator is less than zero, that is, if it is negative. This will be the case if N2 is larger than N1, and a branch will be made to the label LOADN2 (five bytes forward).

At LOADN2, N2 is loaded into the accumulator and the JSR instruction following branches to the monitor subroutine used for displaying the contents of the accumulator in the hex format. The next instruction JMP goes back to re-start the program.

If the BCC test is not true, that is, N1 is larger than N2 (remember they cannot be equal, because this was tested in the previous BEQ instruction) then the instruction following BCC is obeyed. This LDAZ instruction puts N1 into the accumulator, and the JMP instruction following branches to DISPLAY so that N1 is displayed in hex format.

The first byte of each instruction always contains the op code. SED and SEC are one byte *implied* instructions because they only set conditions and do not require operands.

The BEQ and BCC branch instructions refer to relative positions in the program. The op code for these is followed by the number of bytes to be skipped forwards or backwards to reach the next instruction to be obeyed. The number of bytes to be specified in the branch instruction is calculated from the last byte of the BEQ or BCC instruction to the first byte of the instruction to which the

branch is being made. These instructions are two bytes
long. The JMP and JSR instructions require *absolute*
addresses and are three bytes long.

In instructions such as LDX# the operand gives the
actual number to be loaded. The # indicates that the
instruction is of the *immediate* type which is two bytes
long. Other addressing modes used with microprocessors
are outside the scope of this book.

The entry and running of the program given in Table
7.1, on a small 'single-board' microcomputer is described
in the next section.

7.3 Single-board microcomputers

Inexpensive microcomputer systems are commercially
available for educational and industrial use. These systems
can be used for developing simple microprocessor based
programs for a variety of applications, including the
control of electronic and electromechanical models. They
are also useful for teaching machine code programming.

The systems are often referred to as 'single-board'
microcomputers, even though some systems consist of
more than one printed circuit board (PCB). Some manufacturers refer to these systems as microprocessor evalu-
ation systems or microcomputer development modules,
since various hardware devices can be linked to the microcomputers and programs can be developed to control the
devices.

A hexadecimal (or octal) keyboard and LED display may
be mounted on the board together with a microprocessor,
some RAM and input/output ICs. Alternatively, the microcomputer can be interfaced to a visual display unit and/or
typewriter keyboard. Connections come out to the edge of
the board so that edge connectors may be attached. An
interface may be provided for connecting an ordinary
audio cassette recorder, so that programs can be stored on
cassettes and re-entered. Monitoring and control signals

for operating models are transmitted via edge connectors linked to the input/output ICs.

The microcomputers have a monitor program contained in a ROM, which is also on the PCB. This allows entry of programs and data in hex (or octal) codes, and provides various subroutines which can be accessed by the user's program as described in section 7.2. The actual facilities provided vary, and listings are usually given in the user manual that is supplied with each microcomputer system.

Program entry and operation

The operations described are those typically used with small single-board microcomputers. It is assumed that the keyboard contains the full set of hex keys 0–9 and A–F, and some control keys. The availability of the latter and their use is described in the appropriate user manual; the operating concepts given in this section will aid the user to appreciate how programs are entered, edited, saved and executed.

The first step is to connect power to the board by means of the edge connector. This is wired to a small power unit such as a calculator charger, which has a mains transformer outputting 5 to 9v. A voltage regulator may be mounted on the board or the power unit may incorporate this. Connections may also be made to a cassette recorder so that programs may be stored on cassettes, and subsequently read back into the microcomputer. The correct wiring of the edge connectors is shown in the microcomputer's hardware manual or circuit diagram.

The microcomputer is reset to a known state by pressing a reset control key. The program can then be entered into the RAM from the keyboard by keying in the memory addresses and their contents (instruction bytes or data bytes). The address entry mode is selected by pressing the appropriate control key, marked for example as *m* or AD. The required address is then keyed in as a 4-digit hex code and is shown on the LED display. The selected address may be changed by using the hex keys.

The data entry mode is selected by pressing another control key; some systems allow any control key to be used for displaying the contents of the selected memory address, other systems have specially-designated keys, for example, DA. The address contents is entered by pressing two hex digits which comprise one byte. The address contents may be a constant or an instruction or part of an instruction. Each byte of every instruction needs to be entered into the correct memory address.

In data entry mode, the next memory address may be selected by pressing a control key, for example, ∨ or +, which selects the next memory address but does not change the entry mode. The LED display shows the hex code for each memory address as it is selected and the contents, also in hex, when in data entry mode. Some systems allow backtracking of the entries by a control key, for example ∧, which shows the previous address contents, that is the address is decremented by 1. If this facility is not available, then the required memory address is displayed by selecting the address memory mode and entering the hex address; the contents is displayed by selecting data entry mode. Gaps for subsequent insertion of instructions may be left by including NOP ('do nothing') instructions.

Before the program is run, every memory address in the program and its contents should be checked and changed if necessary. This can be done by going back to the start address and displaying each byte in turn, or by backtracking if that facility is available.

The program is executed by giving the microcomputer the start address of the program and pressing the appropriate GO control key. For example, using one system on pressing the control key *g* the microcomputer may display an *h* followed by a 4-digit address; the latter is set to the start address and when any control key is pressed the microcomputer will commence obeying the program instructions starting from the displayed address. On another system, the start address is entered using the AD control key, and execution of the program from this address is initiated when the GO control key is pressed.

If the program execution is not successful, then the cause must be found. A mistake may have been made in entering the program or the logic of the program may be wrong. Detecting such errors is known as debugging and facilities are available in the monitor program to aid this process. Special control keys can be used to allow the contents of the accumulator (A), the X and Y registers, the status register (P), the stack pointer (S) and program counter (PC) to be displayed during execution of the program.

For example, in one system the *p* key enables the user to temporarily replace any byte in the program by a BRK (break) instruction (op code 00). When *p* is pressed P is displayed followed by a 4-digit memory address which can be changed using the hex keys. The contents of the specified address are stored at another special memory address by pressing any control key, and are replaced by 00 so as to put a breakpoint at that place in the program. When the BRK instruction is obeyed the PC and P registers are put on the stack and the contents of the A, X, Y and P registers are displayed in the 8-digit display (two hex digits for each). Pressing any control key causes the contents of the PC and S registers to be displayed (four hex digits for each). These displays allow the programmer to see the results of executing particular instructions or sequences in the program. Pressing the *r* key causes the contents of the PC and P registers to be restored (from the stack) and execution of the program is resumed.

Another system uses a single step facility to execute one instruction at a time. After the execution of any instruction, the contents of the various registers may be displayed by specifying their memory addresses.

When the microcomputer is switched off, the contents of the RAM are lost. Programs may be saved by recording them on cassettes using monitor subroutines and the appropriate store control key. The microcomputer needs to be given the start and end address (one greater than the address of the last byte in the program) of the program to be stored. The program may be loaded back into the microcomputer by pressing a load key, which accesses the tape load subroutine in the monitor program.

7.4 Assembly language programming

Hand assembly of machine code programs involves looking up or remembering the hex (or octal) codes for each op code, working out the memory addresses into which these instructions are to be stored and the addresses used in the instructions. This procedure is slow and error prone.

The assembly process can be carried out automatically using an assembler program. This may be held on a cassette or disk, and the microcomputer will need to have sufficient RAM to hold the assembler program. The assembler translates each instruction in the program, which has been keyed in its mnemonic form (the *source* program), into machine code, and during this process outputs diagnostic information indicating *assembly* errors in the source code. These are not *logical* errors; the latter will not become apparent until the assembled program (the *object* program) is executed.

Some assembly languages incorporate macro instructions for some functions. These macros are used as single instructions but are equivalent to several machine code instructions. The assembler also translates all macros in the program to binary machine code. The assembled listings are usually displayed in hex code next to the assembly language instructions, to make checking easier for the programmer.

7.5   High level languages

Assembly language programs are said to be at the *machine
level*, because apart from any macro instructions, each
source program instruction is equivalent to one machine
code instruction.

Alternatively, *high level* languages may be used, in
which each instruction is generally equivalent to several
machine code instructions. The languages have been
designed to make program writing easier, and they have
facilities which are useful for programming different
applications. Programs written in high level languages are
translated into machine code by interpreters or compilers.

An interpreter is a program which translates one instruction in the source program at a time. The microcomputer attempts to execute the instruction before going
on to translate the next instruction. No complete machine
code version is produced for subsequent loading and
running, so that the source program has to be translated
each time it is used.

A compiler is a program which translates a source
program into machine code *before* it is executed, and
produces a machine code object program. Some compilers
only produce an object program if the compilation has
been successful, that is, no *compilation* errors were found.
Other compilers produce an object program even if there
are certain errors so that the program may be run and give
useful information to the programmer despite the compilation errors, which can subsequently be corrected.
Once a program has been compiled successfully, the
machine code version can be executed whenever required without having to go through the translation process.

The machine code version of the high level language
program may not be as efficient as one written in machine
code or assembly language. An experienced programmer
can optimise the program so that the minimum amount of
storage and processing time is used. However, program

development tends to be much quicker using high level languages.

Universal high level programming languages have been designed for use on many different computers. The choice of language depends on factors such as availability of interpreters and compilers and of standard routines, as well as the processing requirements of the particular application.

One of the first high level programming languages was designed for scientific/engineering applications, as its name implies – FORMULAE TRANSLATOR (FORTRAN). Implementations are available on most computers, including microcomputers, which have sufficient memory to hold the compiler. FORTRAN has been used worldwide for a long time, so that a large library of FORTRAN programs and subroutines is available.

A commonly used programming language for commercial applications is called COBOL (Common Business Oriented Language). This language was designed to handle the data structures required for processing files of business data. It uses English words to describe the data and operations, so as to give some degree of self-documentation. COBOL compilers are large and even the smaller implementations available on some microcomputers require a considerable amount of memory. The majority of commercial applications have been programmed in COBOL. Portability of programs from one computer to another can be a problem, because of different implementations of some of the instructions. However, a COBOL implementation is available which can be used on several different microcomputers.

An alternative to FORTRAN and COBOL was designed originally as a teaching language – Beginners All-purpose Symbolic Instruction Code (BASIC). The language has been considerably extended since its early days, and has become popular for use with small computers, particularly mini- and microcomputers, for both scientific and commercial applications as well as for educational use. The input/output instructions are easy to use compared to those available in FORTRAN and COBOL; however, they have not been implemented in a standard way, so that BASIC programs may have to be modified for use on different computers. The major drawback in using BASIC is that the translation into machine code is often carried out by an interpreter program, so that programs may run too slowly for some applications. BASIC compilers are available on some computers.

Because data has structure, it is desirable that a programming language should reflect this structure. The recognition of this concept has led to structured programming methodologies being developed, and languages have been designed to allow programs to be written in a structured way. A commonly used structured programming language for microcomputers is Pascal. Data in a Pascal program is described as being of a certain type and either variable or constant. The data may be specified as having a certain structure, for example, an array (e.g. list or table) of values. The operations that may be performed on the data can be considered as comprising sequences of statements, which may need to be repeated for a certain number of times, and conditional tests which allow branches to different sequences or repeated sequences (loops) according to the results of each test. Although these operations can be carried out using any programming language, Pascal has been designed to deal efficiently with these structures.

Another high level programming language specially designed for use with small computers is called FORTH. This language comprises a standard vocabulary of 200 words to enable the user to define and create new words which express the logic and relationships required for a particular application. Programs written in FORTH use only a small amount of memory and are fast in execution.

The use of a high level language is illustrated by examples using BASIC, since this is the programming language available on most microcomputers except the smaller single-board microcomputers. The examples have been selected to show how BASIC may be used for scientific, commercial and control applications. BASIC programming and applications are described in *Computer Programming in BASIC*, L R Carter and E Huzan, Teach Yourself Books, 1981.

7.6 Processing experimental data

Programs may be written in BASIC to process experimental data. Although similar calculations may be carried out on a calculator, microcomputers have the advantage of being able to display the information so that the data and results are identified in a clear way.

Some microcomputers are available with graphics facilities. These allow the use of BASIC programs together with special graphics commands to plot points, functions and histograms for different input values. Alternatively, graphics packages are available commercially on cassettes or disks, or the programmer can write routines using the ordinary BASIC commands.

Example

```
10 PRINT "HEAT OF COMBUSTION"
15 PRINT "-------------------"
20 PRINT "NAME OF SUBSTANCE";
30 INPUT N$
40 PRINT "ENTER S,W,T,R";
50 INPUT S,W,T,R
60 LET H=INT(W*4.2*T*R*0.001/S+0.5)
70 PRINT
80 PRINT "RESULT FOR ";N$;" = ";H;" KJ/MOL"
85 PRINT "*********************************"
90 PRINT
100 PRINT "ANY MORE DATA (Y=YES, N=NO)";
110 INPUT Y$
120 PRINT
130 IF Y$ = "Y" THEN 20
140 END
```

Table 7.2 'Heat of combustion' problem

Table 7.2 shows a BASIC program for processing the results of experiments for a class of students. In response to prompts from the computer, each student inputs the name of the substance being investigated, the mass of the substance burnt (S), the mass of water heated by the substance in grammes (W), the rise in temperature of the water in °C (T) and the relative molecular mass (R). The computer calculates the heat of combustion (H) in line 60 of the program (see Table 7.2), and outputs the result. It then asks if there is any more data (line 100) and tests to see if the reply is Y for yes (line 130). If Y is input, the program branches back to line 20 for the next set of data. A typical output together with the data input is shown in Table 7.3.

```
HEAT OF COMBUSTION
------------------
NAME OF SUBSTANCE? ETHANOL
ENTER S,W,T,R? .36,100,23.5,46

RESULT FOR ETHANOL =  1261  KJ/MOL
***********************************

ANY MORE DATA (Y=YES, N=NO)? Y

NAME OF SUBSTANCE? METHANOL
ENTER S,W,T,R? .39,99,21.2,32

RESULT FOR METHANOL =  723  KJ/MOL
***********************************

ANY MORE DATA (Y=YES, N=NO)? Y

NAME OF SUBSTANCE? PROPANOL
ENTER S,W,T,R? .31,101,24.8,60

RESULT FOR PROPANOL =  2036  KJ/MOL
***********************************

ANY MORE DATA (Y=YES, N=NO)? N
```

Table 7.3   Output from Table 7.2 and data input

This method of working is applicable also to, say, a scientist who may perform a number of experiments on different substances and may need to process a series of results using a particular computer program.

7.7 Using data files

Many business applications use data files which have to be set up (created), kept up to date (updated), and used for answering enquiries (interrogated). These files may be held on magnetic tapes or cassettes or magnetic disks. The following simple application illustrates the use of data files using BASIC commands. The input/output commands shown are those typically used with many microcomputers. Some systems may use alternative forms of these commands and reference should be made to the appropriate manual.

A much more sophisticated disk based system is described in chapter 15, section 15.5. This uses the full capabilities of a small business microcomputer.

Example

The data files used in this example consists of a number of stock records. Each stock record contains a stock number (K), item description (D$), stock level (S), unit cost (C) and re-order level (R).

```
10 OPEN 1,1,1,"STK-DATA"
20 INPUT K,D$,S,C,R
30 PRINT#1,K;",";D$;",";S;",";C;",";R
40 IF K=9999 THEN 60
50 GOTO 20
60 CLOSE 1
70 END
```

Table 7.4 Stock data file creation

The program shown in Table 7.4 starts by opening a file "ꜱᴛᴋ-ᴅᴀᴛᴀ" for writing on to a cassette (line 10). The stock records are input from the microcomputer's keyboard one at a time (line 20) and output on to a cassette (line 30). The last record output has 9999 as its stock number; this is a dummy record indicating the end of the file, so that it can be closed (line 60).

```
30 OPEN 1
40 PRINT "RE-ORDER LIST"
45 PRINT "-------------"
50 PRINT
60 PRINT "CODE","DESCRIPTION"
65 PRINT "----","-----------"
70 PRINT
80 INPUT#1,K,D$,S,C,R
90 IF K = 9999 THEN 130
100 IF S > R THEN 80
110 PRINT K,D$
120 GOTO 80
130 CLOSE 1
140 END
```

Table 7.5   Re-order list program

Table 7.5 shows a program which reads each stock record on the cassette in turn (line 80) and outputs the codes and descriptions of the items which need to be re-ordered (line 110). Lines 40 to 70 output two underlined headings followed by a blank line in each case. An example of a re-order list output by this program is shown in Table 7.6.

7.8   Programming a parallel input/output port

A parallel input/output port may be programmed in machine code as shown in chapter 6, section 6.2. Some microcomputers provide instructions which can be used in ʙᴀꜱɪᴄ programs to set the data direction registers (ᴅᴅʀ) and to access the input/output lines.

In the Commodore ᴘᴇᴛ microcomputer, the ᴅᴅʀ for port

```
RE-ORDER LIST
-------------

CODE          DESCRIPTION
----          -----------

    1234      PENS
    2679      ERASERS
    3456      RULERS
    4567      WRITING PADS
    6979      ENVELOPES
    7050      CASH BOOKS
```

Table 7.6 Output from re-order program

A is set by changing the contents of memory address 59459 using a POKE instruction as shown in the following examples:

(a) POKE 59459,255   Sets all bits in port A to 1
                      i.e. to output;

(b) POKE 59459,0   Sets all bits in port A to 0
                      i.e. to input;

(c) POKE 59459,15   Sets DDRA to 00001111
                      i.e. PA7 to PA4 to input
                      and PA3 to PA0 to output.

Any combination of 0s and 1s may be set in the DDR by putting the *decimal* number equivalent to the binary pattern after the memory address in the POKE instruction.

Having set DDRA, the associated port A can be programmed as follows:

POKE 59471, decimal number 0 to 255

results in the lines in port A which are configured as output to be set high or low.

For example, if all the bits in DDRA are set to output as shown in (a), then

POKE 59471,9

will make lines PA3 and PA0 go high so that if LEDs are

attached to all the lines on port A only those on PA3 and PA0 will be switched on.

If the DDRA is now set by POKE 59459,48 (i.e. 00110000) then POKE 59471,9 puts a 0 on PA4 and PA5 the only lines configured as output, and has no effect on the other lines configured as input. Therefore, no LEDs are switched on.

A PET BASIC program can read data input into port A using a PEEK instruction, which examines the contents of memory address 59471.

Example

The example given in Table 6.1, in chapter 6, can be programmed in BASIC for the PET as follows:

BASIC *statements*	*Comments*
10 POKE 59459,48	Set DDRA to 00110000 (LEDs attached to PA4 and PA5, push-button switches on PA0, PA1, PA2 and PA3);
20 INPUT N	Store characters keyed in as binary pattern in memory address N;
30 POKE 59471,0	Set PA4 and PA5 to 0;
40 C=PEEK(59471)	
50 A=C OR 32	Switch on ready light on PA5;
51 A=A AND 32	
60 POKE 59471,A	
70 B=PEEK(59471)	
75 B=B AND 15	Loop until push-button switches are open;
80 IF B <> 0 THEN 70	

BASIC *statements*	*Comments*
90 B=PEEK(59471)	⎫ Loop until at least one
95 B=B AND 15	⎬ switch has been
100 IF B=0 THEN 90	⎭ pressed;
110 FOR I=1 TO 100	⎫ Time delay to allow all
	⎬ selected push-button
120 NEXT I	⎭ switches to be closed;
130 B=PEEK(59471)	⎫
135 B=B AND 15	⎬ Test for correct com-
	bination of switches;
140 IF B <> N THEN 70	⎭
150 C=PEEK(59471)	⎫
155 A=C OR 16	⎬
	Switch on PA4 light.
160 A=C AND 16	
170 POKE 59471,A	⎭
180 STOP	

8   System Development

8.1   Types of system

For every application using microelectronic devices, the associated system also has to be developed. The nature of the work involved allows the required system development to be classified under three broad areas: commercial systems, products and industrial systems.

A feature of commercial systems is that typically the microcomputer is involved with accessing and processing not only direct input via keyboards, etc., but also data and information to be acted upon by those running the organisation. Commercial systems therefore usually use standard microcomputers and the emphasis is on the development of software.

Products such as sewing machines and photocopiers that incorporate microelectronic devices require the system development stage to be part of the product development programme. The system development required involves ensuring that the microelectronic devices are interfaced effectively, via hardware or software, and perform according to specification.

Industrial systems represent an extension of the systems development required for products. Process control, monitoring and analysis require that standard microelectronic based products, such as data loggers and other forms of instrumentation, are combined together with sensors and actuators. The problems encountered are likely to be similar to those experienced in designing a product, but with the added consideration that the system is likely to be unique and not intended for 'mass production'. Development is largely concerned with achieving

satisfactory interfacing either by using proprietary hardware or developing suitable software that may then be put
into ROM.

8.2 Commercial systems development

The development of commercial systems is discussed first
as many of the issues are common to the product and
process applications. Although microcomputer systems
may be smaller and cheaper than conventional 'mainframe computer' systems, the system development required
cannot be similarly scaled down. The steps in developing
and implementing a system still need to take into account
the following aspects:

Systems analysis –
    exploratory study,
    investigation and analysis,
    specification of implementation.
System design –
    systems architecture,
    programming and testing,
    documentation.
Systems implementation –
    file conversion,
    training,
    evaluation and maintenance.

Systems analysis

Commercial applications arise as a result of a user request
or an exploratory study. It is important from the start to
build into the investigation abort stages to prevent any
exploratory study automatically becoming a lengthy and
costly project which is difficult to terminate. Given that
the project passes this point, a more detailed investigation
should then be mounted to allow a systems specification to
be developed.

These investigations provide an opportunity to carry out a thorough analysis of the proposed application. The current system may have evolved over several years and need a complete reappraisal. To simply transfer the current system on to a computer would be a wasted opportunity.

At the end of the systems analysis stage, it should be possible to specify the requirements that the systems design stage needs to meet. It is also necessary, for proper control, to estimate the cost and time schedules to be met by the project group as the application proceeds.

Systems design

The precise relationship between the input system, output system and files needs to be decided before any individual programs can be written. It is convenient to illustrate the architecture of the systems by means of charts in addition to specifying the details of individual sub-systems.

A major consideration at this stage is specifying exactly the format of the input, the output and any information to be held in files. Any subsequent change of these formats is likely in consequence to require the amendment of programs. Manual systems are much more flexible in this respect; figures can be written closer together on a record card or the margin used, but there is no such flexibility automatically built into a computer system. The required flexibility needs to be anticipated and designed in.

Once the architecture and formats have been determined, the necessary programs can be developed almost independently of each other. The programs as they are written need to be debugged and thoroughly tested. The time required to do this should have been adequately estimated at the systems specification stage. Failure to appreciate the time required to test and debug programs often leads to their being released prematurely.

In addition to ensuring the programs do not contain logical errors, safeguards to protect the system from crashing should also be built into the programs. Micro-computer systems in particular are likely to be used by people inexperienced in computers. It is important therefore to ensure that the software disenables all responses other than the correct options from the user. This particularly applies to the Return key whose inappropriate use can take the user out of the program into the operating system.

Despite the opportunity to include remarks and comments in programs all programs should be well documented. Almost any commercial application will require further development at a later stage and it is unlikely that the originators will be on hand to carry out the task. In addition, comprehensive (and comprehensible) documentation needs to be produced for the users of the system.

Systems implementation

Some systems implementation can usually be done concurrently with the programming effort. One major task is the conversion of the existing files. The problem facing management here is that this is a one-off task and furthermore while it is being carried out the existing system must be kept running. Whether the file conversion will be done on overtime, by temporary staff, at a bureau etc., this needs to be planned in advance. In addition, if the level of company activity is seasonal, there may be scope to undertake it during a slack period. The timing of the file conversion activity could well determine the basis of the scheduling of the whole project. Provision also needs to be made for unexpected absence of data in the current system. A manual system will often function normally when a part of the 'data base' is in people's heads. The file conversion stage may show up omissions in the manual system and provision needs to be made to fill these gaps in the computer files.

Concurrently with program writing and file conversion, the plans for training or re-training of personnel needs to be in hand. In addition to deciding the content and extent of the training required, it is also necessary to establish who is to conduct the training. It may be the responsibility of the project team, the company's personnel department, or it may be that outside assistance is more appropriate.

The final stage of the implementation is monitoring the performance of the installed system against the specification. If the system does not perform as expected, then the cause should be determined. Even if the system seems satisfactory an attempt should be made to learn from the project so that future projects are planned even more effectively.

8.3 Packages

Many applications form a common requirement among a large number of users, e.g. sales ledger, mailing systems. In these cases, it is often possible to obtain suites of programs from software organisations. Regardless of the application, the system offered will contain programs to perform the following types of processing:

Create the initial file of data;
Maintain a file by adding new and deleting old records;
Update a file by taking into account file transactions;
Selectively extract information from a file for processing
or output.

The advantages of using supplied programs is that it saves program writing and debugging time. The disadvantage is that their use will be prescribed by the inherent rigidity of pre-written programs. In some cases the programs offered may be too specific, such as a particular method of forecasting; sometimes too general, such as a production control forward load program. To overcome this, some packages allow the user to write routines to link modules of a package to his own programs.

Given that a package is to be used, the associated manual ought typically to contain the following sections:

A description of the computer configuration required;
A résumé of methods used, e.g. forecasting technique;
Input format details;
Output options;
Operating instructions;
Error messages;
An example.

8.4 Development of products and industrial systems

The system analysis and design required for a product, which is to incorporate microelectronic devices, involves both hardware and software skills. Liaison between engineers and programmers needs to be maintained at all stages, and the final product development stages need to be closely co-ordinated.

At an early stage of the system design, decisions need to be made as to which parts of the system will be implemented in hardware and which in software. Either implementation may be feasible and the choice will depend on factors such as cost, the resources available and the time-scale for the project, with respect to both the prototype and the proposed production run.

Industrial systems design is concerned with developing the most effective implementation which gives the required accuracy for monitoring and control of the system's functions.

In the following discussion, both types of system are considered mainly together. A different approach may be needed for particular aspects of the design and implementation.

Systems analysis

The system requirements need to be investigated in detail as for commercial systems. The main difference is that a commercial system is concerned with the processing of data that describes a company's activities, while a product or industrial system is concerned with the processing of digital and analog signals for monitoring and control.

The number of signals, their level and type need to be determined. The interfacing requirements between the microelectronic devices internal and external' to the product/microcomputer need to be identified, at the necessary technical level of detail, to enable the system design to be subsequently carried out.

Section 14.7, in chapter 14, describes the use of a micro-computer control and reporting demonstration model which represents an operational system. This model was developed by the authors and colleagues, and provides examples of the systems analysis aspects that have to be considered.

A schematic of the model is shown in Figure 8.1. The units of resource that flow through the model are brass and steel balls. They are fed from a hopper to the top of the system by a conveyor belt and then roll under gravity down a series of inclined paths back to the hopper. The system needs to control the flow of the balls, count the number of balls to determine when a batch is complete, and count the number of good units (steel) and number of defective units (brass). These three counts need to be transmitted from the controlling and monitoring micro-computer to the reporting microcomputer (see Figure 8.2).

The analysis of the system showed that the reporting microcomputer needs to read three successive bytes of data from its parallel input/output ports and to process these to produce the type of report shown in Table 14.3, chapter 14. The controlling microcomputer needs to:

Start and stop the motor at different stages so that batches of balls are released at required time intervals;

Detect the presence of a ball and determine whether it is brass or steel;

Accumulate the counts;

Send a signal to the reporting microcomputer when it is ready to send data;

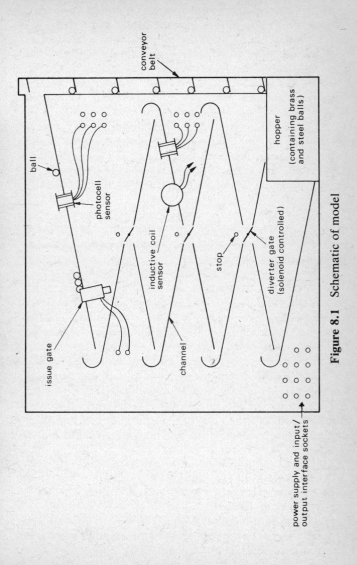

Figure 8.1 Schematic of model

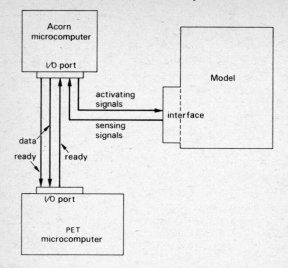

Figure 8.2 Control and monitoring system

Wait for a ready signal from the reporting microcomputer before sending the next byte of data.

This analysis enabled the initial design of the programs to
proceed, but further experimentation with the system was
necessary to obtain precise details of the timing and
control requirements.

It may not be possible to complete the analysis stage
before commencing the design stage and an iterative
approach may be required. At each stage the system
requirements need to be recorded so that the designer has
a comprehensive and precise reference document.

Systems design

The hardware systems designer is involved with the
electronic and electromechanical aspects of the design.
The prototype electronic circuits can be built and tested
using plugboards or breadboards, so that the final layout

can be delayed until the circuits are working correctly.

The software design is carried out concurrently, but not independently, with the hardware design. For example, for the model previously described, the control and reporting programs were designed while problems with the gearing on the motor to control its speed were resolved. However, the design of the control program required a knowledge of the operation of the actuators and detectors used in the model. Factors such as time intervals between opening of gates and the length of time the gates had to be open had to be determined experimentally.

As with a commercial system, different hardware and software has to be investigated so as to determine which is the most suitable for the particular application being developed. However, in some cases more flexibility of choice may be available because of the relatively inexpensive components used in microcomputer control systems. It is less likely that suitable software packages are available for control applications, but the system software (assemblers, compilers, debugging routines) to be used in developing the programs needs to be considered.

The amount of RAM and ROM has to be estimated and a suitable microprocessor/microcomputer system has to be chosen. For product development, it is common to develop the prototype programs using EPROMs so that amendments can be incorporated. The EPROM programs may later be converted to a mask-programmed ROM as described in chapter 4, section 4.2.

There is a choice of alternative strategies that may be adopted for hardware development. It may be decided that because the application is very specialised and/or because of cost considerations the hardware should be built from scratch, using microprocessor, memory and input/output chips (or using a single chip with all these functions), as well as other ICs such as A/D and D/A converters. Alternatively, it may be possible to construct the hardware system from the micromodules which are commercially available.

Some manufacturers supply a full range of micro-modules or systems can be built up from modules supplied by different manufacturers using, say, a standard s100 bus. The types of module available include:

(a)   Microprocessor modules which contain a micro-processor, clock, memory, serial and parallel input/output ports configured as a single-board micro-computer;

(b)   Processor subassemblies which allow the designer to build up a microcomputer with special characteristics;

(c)   Memory modules to allow RAM and ROM to be expanded by the required amount;

(d)   Parallel or serial input/output modules to allow different devices to be interfaced easily;

(e)   A/D and D/A conversion modules for a number of channels and given accuracy.

Alternative strategies are also available for the develop-ment of the hardware/software system. Programs may be developed on stand-alone microcomputers or at terminals attached to a mainframe computer. The latter needs to have an appropriate cross-assembler and cross-compiler.

A cross-assembler is a program which translates an assembly language program on a *different* computer from the one on which it is to be executed. The translated version may be output as a hex listing to be keyed into the microcomputer, or onto paper tape, magnetic tape or disk, or directly into an EPROM. A cross-compiler performs a similar function for programs written in a high-level language.

Various other software development aids are available. Program logic can be checked by using a *simulator*. This is a program which executes the application program being tested one instruction at a time as though the actual micro-processor were being used. However, the execution time of each instruction is likely to be much slower than the actual execution times achieved by the microprocessor, because the simulated execution is carried out by a *soft-

ware routine. This means that any time delays and relationships built into the program can only be tested in the real environment, not by simulation.

This real environment may be emulated using an *emulator* which functions in the same way as the actual microprocessor to be used in the system. The emulator may use the same microprocessor or a different microprocessor. Instruction execution is emulated in *hardware* and correct timings can be achieved.

In circuit emulation (ICE) modules are available which allow hardware and software development to be integrated at an early stage of the project. The ICE module may be plugged into the CPU socket of the user's prototype hardware system to provide microcomputer capabilities. The ICE can also be plugged into its associated Microcomputer Development System to give access to system software. This allows software development to progress before the hardware prototype has been completed. Emulation facilities are often provided as part of the Development System so that timings can be checked.

System implementation

When the prototype system has been fully developed and tested, the final design can be implemented. This may involve building another prototype which has the exact electromechanical and electronic layouts that will be used in the final system. Final testing needs to be carried out to ensure that the proposed product/industrial system will function according to the design specifications.

If the system is a product, detailed engineering drawings are drawn up so that the product can be mass produced. By this time various factors will have influenced the design such as the availability of components currently and in the future, alternative suppliers and cost. The decision to move from EPROM programs to PROM or mask-programmed ROM may not be made at this stage, because the market may need to be tested first.

Full user documentation is required to avoid difficulties in operating the system by inexperienced operators. The documentation needs to be tested by allowing an untrained user to operate the system taking instructions from the user manual.

8.5 Reliability

To design a system to meet an agreed specification it is necessary that each subsystem is designed to a higher standard. Two subsystems, each 90% reliable, will produce a complete system having a total reliability of only 81% (i.e. .9 × .9).

Complex systems, such as computer systems, therefore, need each of their subsystems to be designed to extremely high standards of reliability if the system is to operate in an acceptable manner.

The software needs to be reliable in the sense that:

(a) There are no obscure errors in the logic;
(b) It will always complete its processing in the specified time, regardless of the variety of data input;
(c) It will always 'load' and be executed correctly.

The hardware needs to be reliable with respect to component failure and component deterioration. If two units are interfaced, the reliability of the interface connections constitutes an additional factor and needs to be treated as a part or unit in its own right. When the reliability of particular parts of the system are unacceptably low then extra units may be necessary to provide sufficient redundancy to meet the overall specification.

At the component selection stage, marginal parameter testing may be necessary to establish, say, the permissible voltage variation given a specified current range. A sample of components needs to be assessed as an isolated component may not be representative of a batch. For example, a 0.5 μF capacitor may be on the upper tail of the performance characteristics of 0.5 μF capacitors and its performance may be closer to a typical 0.6 μF capacitor. If only the one 0.5 μF capacitor were checked under circuit condition, the wrong choice would be made.

In general, the normal procedures used in the field of quality control need to be applied to a computer system as for any other designed product or service.

The systems designer also needs to take into account the effect of failure of one part of the system on the rest of the system. The system should be 'insensitive' to failure otherwise a minor fault might cause a cascade effect so that the whole system goes down. In addition to being insensitive to faults, the system should be designed to 'fail' into a 'safe' state. This is not solely a hardware problem but could mean that software needs to be written for this eventuality.

9 Data Communications

9.1 Introduction

The need to transmit information digitally from one electronic device to another in a remote location has led to the extensive development of data transmission systems. This chapter gives a background to data communications and describes some of the terminology and technology that is not covered elsewhere in the book.

9.2 Data communications

Data communications or telecommunications involves the transmission of a signal through media, e.g. wire or air from one electronic device to another. The technologies used in data communications are designed to reproduce the original signal from the source device as faithfully as possible at the best acceptable speed.

The first type of data communication system was the dedicated telegraph line used for the passing of Morse coded signals. Introduction of switched networks led to the widespread use of teleprinters and services such as Telex.

The development of the telephone (analog speech transmission) led to similar networks, dedicated or switched. The normal telephone system being described as a public switched network. For economic reasons telegraph data is often transmitted nowadays over the more extensively developed telephone system. With the growing need to transmit data over switched networks, the distinction between voice and other networks is being lessened. The development of systems needs to take into account that voice and data often share common communication links.

9.3 Transmission of digital data

The changing communication mix has led to increasing use of computers to identify the unused portions of the system to maximise the availability of the channels. Channel capacity has been increased by the application of digital switching.

ICs are available to carry out the specific functions of elements of the traditional communications circuits. For example, the need to follow or correct for any drift in frequency of a carrier wave previously required complex discrete circuitry; this function can now be obtained by using an IC called a phase-locked loop (PLL).

The increase in the transmission of digital data and the advantages of using common communication methods has led to increasing use of Pulse Code Modulation (PCM) as a means of transmitting digitally encoded speech waveforms.

Modulation is the process of altering the characteristics of a carrier wave in accordance with the characteristics of another wave or signal. The resultant composite waveform is the modulated signal. Carrier wave characteristics can be modulated in several ways. In radio broadcasting, for example, the two most common ways are to alter the amplitude of the carrier wave (amplitude modulated, AM) or to alter the frequency of the carrier wave (frequency modulation, FM).

Frequency Shift Keying (FSK)

Frequency shift keying is a method of modulating a signal by changing the frequency. As the signal consists of a series of coded pulses (high or low), referred to as marks and spaces respectively, the carrier frequency is shifted up or down by a fixed amount. One standard uses a shift of

85 Hz (i.e. ± 42.5 Hz either side of the carrier frequency).
   Frequency shift keying is a particular form of frequency modulation.

Pulse modulation

Pulse modulation is a form of modulation in which information is conveyed by altering some parameters in a train of pulses. Thus as before the amplitude can be

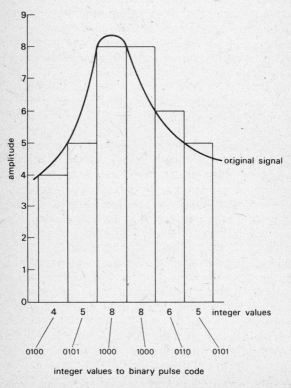

Figure 9.1   Analog signal to pulse code

modulated (pulse amplitude modulation, PAM) or the frequency (PFM) etc.

Pulse coded modulation is a particular form of pulse modulation whereby only certain discrete values are allowed for the modulating signal. Each value is assigned a pattern of pulses and the signal transmitted is this pulse code (see Figure 9.1).

Morse code is an early example of manually generated pulse code modulation. Modern PCM, as used to transmit data or speech equivalent between devices, contains a greater range of codes and operates at a much faster rate than manually transmitted Morse code.

In AM or FM a parameter of the modulated wave varies continuously during transmission. In pulse modulation, the pulses are of such short duration that the pulse modulated wave is off most of the time. This allows the time between the pulses to be filled with samples of other data streams. The multiplexity of several pulse modulations in this manner is known as Time Division Multiplexing (TDM).

A further feature of pulse code modulation is that it allows the infinite repetition of the signal through repeaters without any cumulative signal degeneration. At each repeater the signal can be completely and accurately reformed for onward transmission (see Figure 9.2).

9.5 Modems

Modems (modulator-demodulators) are used to modulate the signal at the source of the data transmission and to de-modulate the signal at the receiving end. The modem's modulation technique can vary as explained previously, but in use both modems at each end of the communication link must be compatible.

When data is transmitted serially via modems, there are two methods of transmission, asynchronous and synchronous, as briefly described previously in chapter 6, section 6.3.

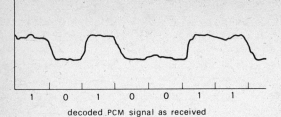

decoded PCM signal as received

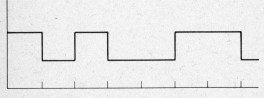

reformed PCM signal as sent on

Figure 9.2   Reformation of PCM signal

Asynchronous transmission

With modems using this method of transmission, each character is preceded by a 'start' bit which wakes up the receiver. The character is followed by at least one 'stop' bit to allow both transmitting and receiving devices to be ready for the next character.

The function of the start bit is to allow the oscillators (clocks) at both ends to be synchronised. Even though the clocks might not be precise (e.g. differing by say 2Hz at 1200 Hz), they will not become seriously out of phase during the transmission of one character. The stop bit allows the clocks to be reset.

Synchronous transmission

The stop-go nature of asynchronous transmission makes it only suitable for low speed communications, not above, say, 1800 baud.

Synchronous transmission involves sending a continuous stream of bits from a buffer after having initially sent a string of synchronising data. If the data stream stops, it must be resynchronised but a continuous stream allows anything from 1000 to 10,000 bits to be transmitted before resynchronisation becomes necessary.

Low speed modems usually use FSK, transmitting a 1070 Hz frequency to represent a 0 and 70 Hz for a 1.

High speed modems transmitting at, say, 4800 baud use multilevel phase modulation. One system represents three consecutive data bits by one of eight phase angles (60, 120, 150, 210, 240, 300, 330, 30 degrees representing 000, 001, 010, . . . 111 respectively).

9.6 Fibre optic communication

The traditional means of transmitting information and data electronically is by the use of copper wires. With the advent of radio and satellite stations, data may be transmitted over great distances without a physical link. A third important option has become possible with the development of microcircuit lasers, that is, fibre optics. Fibre optic communication has several advantages over copper wire.

Transmission of signals through copper wire has several limitations. As the transmission losses increase with the information rate, there is an upper limit on the number of 'simultaneous' transmissions that can be carried by a pair of copper wires. Some improvement can be obtained by using co-axial copper cables but they are more bulky. Copper wires are also susceptible to electromagnetic interference from nearby devices (and lightning). Copper transmission wires create magnetic fields and adjacent wires may pick up some of the signals (cross-talk). Signals sent over distance by wire need to be amplified by repeaters at about two km intervals. Lastly, there is the problem of avoiding copper corrosion under certain environmental conditions.

None of the above problems exists with fibre optics, mainly because light does not create a magnetic field. The number of repeaters is less – approximately one every six km – and glass fibre does not corrode.

The data is transmitted as a stream of infra-red photons emitted from semi-conductor lasers. The increase in traffic using fibre optics is of the order of 10,000 times that of copper wire.

Lasers

Laser stands for *l*ight *a*mplification by the *s*timulated *e*mission of *r*adiation, and produces an intense radiation over a narrow frequency band.

The gallium arsenide (GaAs) laser is a solid state laser. The radiation is due to the electrons from the n-region dropping into the holes of the p-region at the p-n junction. To produce the laser action it is necessary to build up this radiation along the plane of the junction. This is achieved by creating a highly polished face perpendicular to the junction (see Figure 9.3).

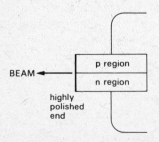

Figure 9.3   A solid state laser

The main application for fibre optics is in replacing the copper wires that carry the communications between one switching centre and another. However, a reported application in the US Navy enabled 1900 ft of copper wire (weighing 30 lbs) on an aircraft to be replaced by 224 ft of fibre optics weighing 1.52 lbs. The reduction in weight and space being a significant factor in an aircraft installation.

In certain applications where security is important, fibre optics have the advantage of being difficult to tap, as no magnetic field exists. Any tapping necessitates direct splicing which can then be detected from the signal loss.

9.7 Facsimile (FAX)

FAX is the process of scanning graphic material to produce an electrical signal. The transmitted signal is then reconverted to produce a likeness to the original. The process has been used for many years by newspapers (for photographs) and shipping (for weather maps).

The move towards digitising the transfer of information has enbled facsimile machines to operate at higher speeds and with improved quality. The copy to be transmitted is scanned line by line by a laser light source. Reflected light (or shade) is picked up by a solid state photoreceptor. The signal is then modulated prior to transmission.

Depending upon the quality and speed required, the more elaborate FAX machines have the lines per inch switch selectable. Each line comprises approximately 1700 print elements which are digitised into black or white for transmission. As much of the document is white, the digitised information includes codes to skip to black areas. Using this approach, a typical A4 document can be transmitted in about 35 seconds.

The received signal is demodulated and applied to a laser whose output varies in line with the original. This light beam is then used to reproduce a copy using traditional xerography.

FAX is particularly useful for the transmission of engineering and architectural drawings and in banking for the transmission of signed authorisations.

9.8   Line codes and protocols

To connect different makes and types of device, and pass streams of binary codes between them, it is necessary that the devices work to some coding convention. Thus any digital coding system needs to include a range of control character codes in addition to being able to represent numeric, alphabetic and the usual special characters, e.g. %, @.

There are a number of codes in use today. The code developed for teleprinter and telegraphy is the CCITT Alphabet No 2 code (commonly called 'Baudot' code or 'Murray' code). This code is constructed from five bits and is too limited for use in computers. In so far as transmissions use this code, it is necessary for the computer to translate the incoming line code to its internal code.

The need to have a code containing more characters and hence more bits led to various 7-bit codes being developing by different manufacturers. This led to the development of the more widely used ASCII code (see also Appendix B).

Some of the ASCII control character codes are shown in Table 9.1. The way they are used to create a dialogue between communicating devices is known as the line protocol.

code	character	meaning
0000010	STX	start of text
0000011	ETX	end of text
0000100	EOT	end of transmission
0000101	ENQ	request for response (enquiry)
0000110	ACK	positive acknowledgement
0010101	NAK	negative acknowledgement

Table 9.1   Some ASCII control character codes

When only two devices are involved the point to point protocol is known as 'contention' line control. The sequence used is started by the transmitting device sending an ENQ character, and waiting for 1–5 seconds. Normally the response time is milliseconds. Failure to acknowledge within the allowed time frame leads to a 'time out' and an appropriate message is generated to the user. Normally, an ENQ results in the receiving device replying ACK (yes, carry on transmitting) or NAK (no, not able or ready to receive).

The transmission is then started by STX, followed by the data, ending with ETX and BCC (Block character check). The block checking character is a form of parity check for the whole block of code transmitted. If this check is successful, the receiver responds with ACK otherwise it sends NAK and waits for a re-transmission of the data.

If two devices are linked, the problem of both sending ENQ codes simultaneously is overcome by having their timeout clocks set to slightly different values. If they happen to send ENQ together, one will timeout before the other and 'get in first'.

In conversational mode, the sending of ACK after a block of data is taken as the receiver's readiness to accept more.

When many terminals are connected to a central computer, the protocol requires the computer to 'poll' each device in turn to ascertain whether there is anything to send. Each device as it is polled in turn responds with EOT, if there is nothing to transmit. Devices that are not connected or turned on, and therefore do not respond, are timed out as previously explained.

The above describes the basis of line protocols. In practice, the sequence of codes may be more complex and dependent on the particular hardware used. For example, a particular system uses a special control character WAK, which if sent in acknowledgement of a data block, means 'data acceptable, but do not send any more yet'.

9.9   PABX **(Communications system)**

The development of digital switching techniques has led
to the traditional telephone switchboard being completely
redesigned using such techniques. This has also resulted in
the range of communication facilities offered being considerably enhanced. The 'telephone switchboard' has
been replaced by a 'communications system'.

The basis of the change is twofold:

(a)   The digitising of the speech using pulse coded modu-
      lation (PCM);
(b)   The use of time division multiplexing (TDM) switch-
      ing to allow a high traffic density over a common
      digital bus.

As a result of digitising and having microprocessor
control over the switching a large number of facilities can
be offered to the users of a telephone system. Typical
facilities might include:

1   *Call waiting*
When a second caller dials a 'phone already in use, a LED
at the receiving station flashes, alerting the user to the
situation. The user may then opt to hold the first call and
take the second, returning to the first call when he wishes.

2   *Conference*
To set up a 'conference' by 'phone, the initiator pushes a
conference key before dialling each party in turn. All the
numbers dialled are then interconnected simultaneously.
This feature is usually limited to six parties.

3   *Route restriction*
General access may be denied to certain extensions;
access can only be obtained from certain specified stations.

4   *Power failure reload*
All data in the systems memory is duplicated on magnetic

backing store so that when power is restored after a power failure, the system is restored automatically.

5 *Call pick-up*
An extension user can opt to 'answer' another 'phone within a pre-designed group by pushing a 'call pick-up' key on his unit or by dialling an allocated code.

6 *Automatic dialling*
An extension user can assign frequently dialled numbers to one of a number of pre-set keys. The numbers can be re-assigned as required by the user.

7 *Call forward*
Calls to any extension can automatically be forwarded on to another extension. This action is initiated by the receiving extension activating call forward mode and dialling the extension number from which calls are to be re-routed.

8 *Ring again*
This feature indicates to a calling station when a busy number becomes available. Connection is then made by pushing the 'ring again' key without re-dialling.

Telephone answering machines

Telephone answering machines are a useful way of receiving calls when the telephone has to be left un-attended. Microprocessor-controlled answering machines can offer more sophisticated facilities by allowing a remote unit to transmit codes into the 'answering' machine to control its operation. This allows the answering machine to be controlled from any telephone in the world. The remote unit can initiate the playback of previously recorded messages, can rewind the answering machine tape for as many repetitions as required and can erase messages no longer required.

Microprocessor intercoms

Intercoms having microprocessors built into each station do away with the need for a costly central exchange, so that subsequent expansion of the system is simple.

Regardless of the number of stations each is connected to common wiring. The built-in microprocessor at each station performs the necessary switching and connecting for that station. By this means the normal intercom facilities of conference calls (i.e. several stations interconnected simultaneously) and transferring calls can be achieved. This type of intercom can also be developed to act as a remote switching device, to activate surveillance systems and other building services.

10 Aspects of Instrumentation

10.1 Introduction

This chapter discusses some of the aspects of instrumentation in relation to the linking of equipment into industrial processes and laboratory experiments.

A brief overview of transducers is given by describing some of the types available and then by considering the ways in which one parameter (water level) could be measured.

An example of digital encoding methods is given together with the reasons why the natural binary system needs to be amended for this area of application.

The way in which transducers of the above type can provide input to a data logging system is covered with the associated aspects of multiplexing and application of analog to digital converters.

10.2 Transducers

Transducers are devices that respond to some change in a physical quantity by giving a change in their output signals. For the purposes of this book, only signals related to changes in electronic parameters are considered, although the varying output signal may, in other types of transducers, be air or liquid pressure.

The transducer forms the sensor of a monitoring system, e.g. car engine temperature is registered on a meter that obtains its signals from a temperature sensitive transducer suitably located in the engine coolant.

It is important in choosing transducers to ensure that the presence of the transducer does not affect the situation being monitored or that its presence does not affect the values being measured. For example, a temperature sensor might conduct heat away at such a rate that the process being monitored is affected, or the temperature becomes lower than that attained without a sensor present.

Other general considerations in using transducers are:

Accuracy
It is necessary to ensure that the accuracy of the transducer is within acceptable limits for the application.

Resolution
This is the term used for defining the fineness to which a measurement can be made. A device might be capable of high resolution but still be inaccurate.

Hysteresis
The output from the transducer may depend upon the direction from which it has changed, high to lower, or low to higher. The hysteresis is the amount by which the measurand (variable being measured) can be changed (in the opposite direction) before the output indicates a change.

Hysteresis is often quite marked with the thermostat of a central heating system. A progressive fall, say, in temperature is signalled accurately to the central heating pump, degree by degree, but a 5° rise in temperature may be necessary before the pump shuts down.

Repeatability
This is the closeness of agreement of consecutive readings obtained after full range traverses of the measurand.

Linearity
A knowledge of the linearity or otherwise of the output in response to changes in the measurand is necessary. Non-linearity can often be compensated for in subsequent processing of the signal.

Response time
The time taken by the output of the transducer to respond to changes in the measurand can be important if a situation is to be monitored effectively.

10.3 Types of transducer

There is a vast range of transducer devices, many being designed for specific purposes. Thus loudspeakers, microphones, record player pick-up heads, are all examples of commonly found transducers. For industrial processes and instrumentation applications, transducers are used for the measurement of speed, pressure, temperature, etc. and it is transducers associated with these areas that will be considered here.

Movement can be measured through inductive transducers and smaller movements, particularly pressure, through piezoresistive and piezoelectric transducers. Temperature can be measured through thermocouples and thermistors.

Inductive transducers
One type of inductive transducer will be described, the linear variable differential transformer (LVDT). An LVDT consists of a primary and two secondary coils on a common former. The primary coil is energised continuously which causes the voltages in the secondary coils to change whenever the core moves (in response to pressure or a mechanical linkage). The two secondary coils are connected in series, such that when the core is in its neutral position the net difference between the voltage in both coils is zero. Displacement of the core causes the net difference to increase linearly with the movement and to be in phase or out of phase with the primary according to the direction of movement.

Potentiometric transducers
By coupling a potentiometer in a suitable manner with the movement to be monitored the change in resistance can

be measured. The relationship may be linear or otherwise depending upon the resistive windings on the potentiometer.

Strain gauges

Small degrees of movement and force can be detected by strain gauges. Thin film techniques allow strain gauges to be produced as printed circuits. Semi-conductor strain gauges based upon the piezoresistive effect are made by connecting two crystals in series but giving each crystal different impurities. This leads to the gauge being temperature compensated, the effect of a temperature change on one crystal being cancelled out by the other crystal.

Piezoelectric transducers

Piezoelectric crystals and materials (e.g. lead-zirconate-titanate ceramics) are polarised. Man-made ceramics can be moulded into any shape and the direction of polarisation built in during production. If the crystal or ceramic is 'squeezed' in a particular direction, a voltage is produced.

Thermocouples

Thermocouples develop a voltage that is proportional to the temperature difference between their hot and cold junctions of dissimilar metals. Typical metals are Iron/Constantan or Platinum/Platinum-Rhodium.

Thermistors

Thermistors are semi-conductors whose resistance changes with the temperature. Typical materials are sintered oxides of magnesium, nickel, copper and they can be formed into rods, beads or wafers.

As an example of the range of options and alternatives that need to be considered in choosing transducers, some different ways of measuring fluid level will be described.

10.4 Fluid level detectors

A common principle used is to fix a number of sensors down a column containing the fluid. The physical size of the sensors determines the resolution that is obtained.

The presence of fluid can be detected in a number of ways. Conductance between two coils will change in the presence of certain fluids. Possibly a more widely applicable method, that can also be used with free flowing powders, is to use capacitors as sensors. The principle is illustrated in Figure 10.1.

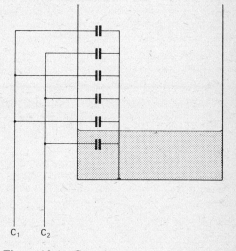

Figure 10.1 Capacitor sensors for fluid level

When the fluid is low, no capacitor is shorted out by the fluid, and $C_1 = C_2$. As the fluid level rises and shorts out the lowest capacitor, then $C_1 > C_2$. Rising further, the next capacitor is also shorted out bringing the two capacitance circuits into balance again, i.e. $C_1 = C_2$. If the two sets of capacitance are coupled to a capacitance bridge, the output can be a voltage or zero as $C_1 > C_2$ or $C_1 = C_2$ respectively. The voltage can give rise to a logic '1'.

Thus as the fluid rises or falls, the resultant series of signals will be alternate 0s or 1s which can be encoded by circuitry as required.

The drawback with the above approach is that the sensors are discrete. In some application, the fluid level can be monitored by means of a probe consisting of a pair of stainless steel wires, say, 1.5mm diameter and 12mm apart. The electrical conductivity between the wires is linearly related to their depth of immersion.

A further method of monitoring the fluid level is to use a pressure sensitive transducer at the bottom of the vessel. The fluid, under pressure from its own weight, enters the transducer and deforms a diaphragm. The degree of deformation can be monitored by a strain gauge attached to the diaphragm.

10.5 Angular Digital Encoders (ADE)

The transducers described so far all produce an analog output. As an example of other types of measurement, this section describes a means of monitoring angular movement by means of a digital encoder.

Angular digital encoders can be extremely accurate; those giving a 20-bit binary output can represent 1 second of an arc. However, the cost of obtaining this precision means that a range of methods exist depending upon the precision/cost constraints.

Absolute encoders

Absolute encoders give a complete digital readout in any position and are based upon an encoding disc which is coupled directly to the angular position being sensed. The disc may be read by brushes making direct contact with a metallic coding pattern, by toroidal magnetics picking up a magnetic pattern on the disc, or by optical methods using photoelectric principles.

Scanning problems, particularly using brush contacts, can arise using natural binary code. For example, in advancing from 011 to 100 all sensors need to change simultaneously. If any sensor is 'out of line' several erroneous outputs are generated. To overcome this problem, cyclic binary codes have been developed. A cyclic binary code is designed so that only one bit changes at a time, one common system being the Gray code. An example of the Gray code is given below:

decimal	Gray code
0	0000
1	0001
2	0011
3	0010
4	0110
5	0111
6	0101
7	0100
8	1100
9	1101
10	1111

The rules for converting Gray code to natural binary are as follows:

(a) Leave the most significant bit (MSB);
(b) For other bits, if the number of 1s to the left is even, leave unchanged, otherwise change.

For example:

Gray code:	1 0 1 1
MSB unchanged	1 – – –
Number of bits to left odd, change	– 1 – –
Number of bits to left odd, change	– – 0 –
Number of bits to left even, no change	– – – 1
Natural binary	1 1 0 1

It can be seen from the above that suitable logic circuits, or programming, can be used to convert from Gray to natural binary code or vice-versa.

Incremental encoders

Incremental encoders determine in digital form the angular position of a shaft relative to some datum. They generate a fixed number of pulses for each unit of angular rotation. The disc usually has three tracks, a count track, a direction track and a datum track.

The count track contains the segments to be counted by the sensor and counting circuits. The direction track consists of similar segments to the count track but are out of phase by a fixed amount. In one direction of rotation the direction track signals will therefore lead the count track signals, while in the opposite direction they will lag. Logic circuitry can therefore determine from this the direction of rotation. The signal (pulse) from the datum track acts as a reset on the counter.

Digital tachometers

A basic application of angular digital encoders is to measure velocity by, for example, counting the number of pulses received over a clocked period of time.

The circuits adopted can be based upon either absolute or incremental encoders. However, if a cheap and simple transducer is required for speed measurement, it might be possible to take advantage of an existing toothed wheel on the shaft. If there is a toothed wheel, an electromagnetic solenoid can be placed in proximity to the rotating teeth. The passage of the teeth will induce pulses in the coil.

10.6   Multiplexers

The multiplexer's function is to switch the appropriate transducer into the circuitry. With analog signals there may be the need to use up to three switches in parallel (3-pole), two for the analog signal and a third for common grounding the earth.

There are three main types of multiplexer: mechanical rotary, electromagnetic and transistor.

Mechanical rotary switching comprises a rotating arm that carries contacts to connect to, say, 25 contacts on a fixed disc. The arm and disc often have three sets of contacts allowing a 3-pole switching action. The arm can be driven by a motor and its position is obtained from a coded contact disc as BCD output.

Electromagnetic switching usually takes the form of reed switches, which consist of a pair of contacts in a sealed glass tube. The contacts are closed by energising a solenoid around the tube. It is also possible to obtain reed switches housed in integrated packages. Activation of the switches is from the control logic of a computer. The control signal, in BCD, is passed to an address decoder which provides a logic '1' to the chosen channel (reed switch).

The speed of reed switching is largely limited by the noise generated from the contact bounce. Variations on the reed switch have led to diaphragm relays whereby contact in the glass tube is made by a ferrous diaphragm being attracted to a metal core. This type of relay is less liable to bounce and is more resistant to shock and vibration.

Because of the limitations of these essentially electro-mechanical devices, there is some advantage in using transistor circuitry for switching. The sampling speed of a transistor multiplexer switch is considerably higher (measured in MHz, compared to 500 operations per second for reed switches).

10.7 Digital data logging

Digital data logging requires the instrumentation to detect a signal by means of a transducer and to convert the resultant measurement into a digital form, so that it can be displayed or recorded or interfaced with a general computer system.

The logging operation often involves accessing the output of several transducers in sequence. This gives rise to a multiplexing arrangement. As each part of the logger needs to be kept synchronised, there is the need for a timing and control section.

The output from a transducer would usually need to pass through a signal conditioning circuit to 'clean up' the signals, it may then require amplifying so that it is of a sufficient level to be processed through an analog to digital converter (A/D), (see also chapter 6, section 6.6).

There are several ways of linking a number of transducers to a common computer system. In an analog multiplexer system, multiplexer circuits are inserted between the analog inputs and the single A/D converter. A command from the central processor via the address logic decoder causes a particular analog input to be switched through the multiplexers. The signal is suitably conditioned (i.e. filtered and amplified). Control signals, from the central processor, sample and hold the signal and initiate the A/D converter. The sampled digital equivalent is then read into the computer memory.

When there are not many transducers to be sampled, the use of multiplexers can be avoided at the expense of running multicore cable to decoders and switches associated with each transducer. The central processor, in this case, sends out a digital code along the address highway (bus) which is recognised by the appropriate decoder and causes its transducer to be switched on to a common data highway. The signal on the data highway is then conditioned and passed through an A/D converter as before. A possible source of problems with this system is the fact that all the transducers are connected to a common data highway and the nature of the analog signals could cause interactions.

To overcome the above problem, a further variation is to have A/D converters associated with each transducer so that the data highway carries digital signals.

A block diagram showing a method of linking transducers to a central processor via digital multiplexing is shown in Figure 10.2.

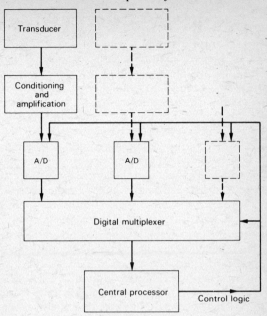

Figure 10.2   A method of linking transducers to a
central processor

NIC

When analog signals are being handled, additional unwanted signals can become present. Depending on the
nature of the equipment the unwanted elements may be
'picked up' or self-induced. The unwanted signals can be
classified as noise, interference and crosstalk (NIC).

Noise is an all-embracing term to cover any unwanted
aspect of the received signal. It is often introduced due to
power surges or switching transients from associated
equipment. Interference is 'picked up' often at harmonics.
Crosstalk arises from the coupling of a signal from one
source into another.

The best means of avoiding NIC is prevention, the most

effective way being to treat the source. Leads need to be shielded and if necessary twisted. As far as possible, multiple earthing of equipment should be avoided.

11 Industrial Applications

11.1 Introduction

This chapter discusses some of the many and varied applications of microcomputers in industry. The microcomputer is interfaced to the industrial system by the use of suitable transducers as described in the previous chapter.

A major application is in the control of machine tools. Numerically controlled (NC) equipment has developed rapidly as the result of microprocessors. The need to link and feed machine centres has given rise to microcomputer applications in the field of robotics.

Process control in general has become technically feasible in almost every instance, the appropriateness of any application depending upon the economics of the case. The direction in which one pharmaceutical company is moving as a result of microelectronic technology is described.

Even after the product has been produced there are further stages such as packaging, labelling and wrapping. A labelling system is described that allows on-line or off-line programming.

In any company quality is important and the need to measure and test is always present. Some microprocessor applications in this area are given followed by a description of an application in an analytical laboratory.

11.2 Machine tools

Machine tools are a class of metal removing machines such as lathes, millers and drillers. The basis of the cutting process is the movement of the cutting tool in relation to the material in a precise orientation and by a precise amount. Traditional numerical control (NC) is based upon the movement being controlled via a pre-prepared punched paper tape. The development of microprocessors and compact computers has extended the sophistication of the control available, so that the term computer numerical control (CNC) is used. A diagram of the basic control system is shown in Figure 11.1. For simplicity, only one controlled movement is shown. In practice, movements in all three dimensions are controlled.

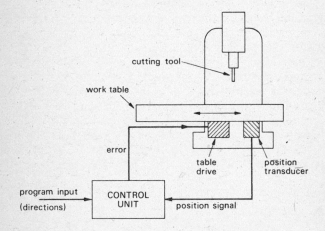

Figure 11.1 Basic numerical control system

The actual movement and monitoring of the controlled axes are carried out by motors and position transducers respectively.

On the above basis numerical control machine tools have been used for many years prior to the development of microelectronics. The application of microcomputers allows for more sophisticated control. When metal is machined its cutting properties can vary throughout the workpiece, particularly if it is a forging or casting. Microcomputers can add a further aspect of adaptive control by reacting to the current power consumption, torque, etc. of the driving motors.

Due to the nature of microcomputer systems a distributed processing approach can be adopted for the control of the various functions of a machine tool. This also allows a modular approach to the development of the hardware and software. In addition, greater operator interaction for unexpected situations is possible due to the work cycle not being restricted to pre-programmed punched paper tape.

Instead of being a substantial part of the cost of a machine tool, the use of microcomputers makes the numerical control cost less and adds relatively little to the cost of the machine tool.

Some control systems are too complex for a single microprocessor. One approach is to use a bit slice microprocessor system whereby the codes on the data bus are broken into slices, each having the same number of bits (i.e. 16 bits into 4 slices of 4 bits). Each of the slices is then processed in separate processors.

An alternative to bit slice microprocessors for complex systems is to use several microprocessors together. An

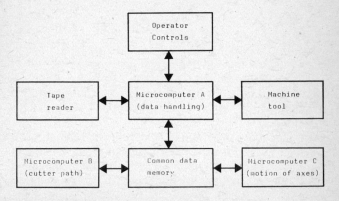

Figure 11.2 A multi-microcomputer system

example of this is shown in Figure 11.2. Microcomputer A acts as a programmable interface between the machine tool and the system. It also handles tape and operator input and output. Microcomputer B calculates the axes motions as a function of time and hence the path of the cutter, and microcomputer C controls the position of the feed axes. The three microcomputers share a common data memory. As more microcomputers are linked to the machine a greater on-line processing capability is built up. For example, 'worksurface programming' is the technique whereby the desired profile of the workpiece is specified and the size of the blank is entered. The control system works out the pattern of cuts necessary to produce the component. In some cases, this is displayed on a VDU as a check before the operator commits the machine.

The addition of VDUs to machine tool control systems allows a conversational approach which guides the operator when inputting the required data. The use of microcomputers has enabled the development of digital readout systems (with memory). The current position of all co-ordinates is displayed and in some cases the display can be switched at any time from Imperial units to metric and vice-versa.

11.3 Robots

The term robot tends to be used for a class of computer-controlled machines that follows a programmable pattern of behaviour. They are used, for example, as automatic handling devices for paint spraying and welding.

Automatic handling devices typically have up to six axes of control, three axes of motion in the 'hand' for picking or placing the workpiece, three axes of motion to move the workpiece. Five axes of rotation can effectively simulate a human operator's waist, shoulder and elbow rotation, wrist bend and hand rotation. One robot of this type can load up to five numerical control machines grouped around it; similar types can load a lathe.

The simplest and earliest type of robot was a fixed sequence type. Once set up to do a job they perform it repeatedly. To perform a different sequence they need re-programming. This is often done by the operator moving the robot's 'hand' through the desired sequence, the sequence being recorded in computer memory. In some cases, the sequence can be off-loaded on to tape for storage and subsequent use.

The type of robot control used can be classified as either point to point (ptp) or continuous path (cp). Ptp systems do not control the path between the specified points and are typically used in such applications as spot-welding. Cp systems implement a smooth continuous movement and as a consequence are more sophisticated and costly.

A fixed sequence robot relies on the part to be handled, sprayed, etc. to be in the correct position. If the part is missing the robot will either stop or carry on handling 'thin air'. The typical precision attained is the arm repeating its movement to within 0.1 mm. The load that can be handled is about 4 kg.

The developments in robotics is towards adaptive robots having sensory abilities. Initially the requirement is for robots to have a sense of vision and touch. This will allow a robot to identify the correct part among dissimilar items and pick it up regardless of its position. Robots of this type are being introduced into assembly lines.

The theoretical basis of the work needed to develop sophisticated adaptive robots is referred to as 'Artificial Intelligence' (AI). A robot's ability to 'see', for example, is a problem in 'pattern recognition'. Problems in this area are concerned more with developing suitable software rather than with building suitable robots.

Although this discussion has centred on industrial robots, robots and robotic principles are being increasingly used in unmanned space missions, and in deep ocean diving equipment.

11.4 Process control

The control of processes in general is a wider extension of the principles used in numerical control of machine tools. Instead of monitoring and controlling solely movement, other parameters such as temperature, time, gas flow, etc. are monitored and controlled. The possibilities are endless, provided suitable transducers exist for the parameters to be controlled. Provided this is the case, the more complex the process the more suitable it is for microcomputer control.

Efficient operation of furnaces is an example where energy savings can be substantial when the process is properly controlled. A microprocessor-based system can monitor signals from thermocouples, air-flow meters, fuel flow meters and gas analysers, and on the basis of heat loss calculation and furnace efficiency optimise the fuel/air ratio.

In an application such as this, it is also possible to collect information of the furnace performance over time. An analysis of this information provides a valuable guide to damage and wear and to establishing the time for appropriate corrective maintenance.

Another heat dependent process is injection moulding. A microcomputer can monitor melt temperature, die temperature, pressure, cooling time, etc. to control the cycle in accordance with the specification of the material being used.

In practice, despite theoretical laws, many industrial process parameters are chosen and varied according to company accumulated data and operator judgement. This can lead to erratic production and quality problems. With microcomputer control systems, this data can be stored and drawn upon from computer memory leading to greater uniformity of output.

The calculation of optimum tool life from theoretical laws, for example, is not practical because of the variations in the properties of the actual workpiece. Optimum tool life more realistically should be based upon actual experience. It is feasible nowadays to monitor and analyse data to recalculate continuously optimum tool life.

Continuous monitoring of vibration in machinery allows the vibration pattern to be analysed. Any abnormal wear or breakdown of bearings will show up as a dramatic change in the pattern of vibration.

11.5 Pharmaceutical applications

In this type of work, accuracy of recording is essential, first to ensure mistakes are not made, and secondly to enable a particular consignment to be traced back through the production processes identifying the equipment lines and the raw material batches of its origin.

The issue of raw materials can be controlled and recorded effectively by using light pens to monitor and check bar codes on raw material containers when the material is issued for weighing. The scales of the weighing system can also be controlled to check against pre-recorded formulation. The stock quantity can automatically be adjusted from the weighing station once an 'accept' command is issued by the operator.

There is also scope to apply microcomputers to the production process. For example, a typical process might require 'sintering' of the raw material whereby it is granulated, heated and cooled. A microcomputer controlled system can monitor the moisture content of the materials, monitor and adjust the temperature and cooling rate and determine the optimum time for the 'baking' and cooling.

To control this type of operation manually means that one either relies on experienced operators or that extensive statistical analysis is carried out by a quality control section. The results of quality control can then be fed back to alter the process parameters in a formal manner using a technique known as evolutionary operations (EVOP). An on-line microcomputer controlled system can implement the equivalent of an EVOP approach in a much more effective manner.

11.6   A labelling system

There are many situations that call for labels to be applied to products, packs or packages. One development is that of a matrix imprinter that allows the in-line printing of self-adhesive labels just prior to application. A keyboard allows easy direct operation but variable data can also be easily pre-programmed in advance of printing. For continuous in-line labelling applications the required text, bar codes or OCR characters can be pre-programmed. The system consists of five modules:

> Printer module,
> Data entry (keyboard and VDU),
> Mini-floppy disk unit,
> Microcomputer,
> Interface unit.

Altogether the system can operate in three modes:

1   As a totally integrated on-line overprinting system, adding variable information to labels immediately prior to application;
2   As an on-line or off-line variable overprinting system whereby the input data is received from a computer;
3   As an on-line printing system where the data was pre-programmed off-line for subsequent label applications.

11.7   Inspection and measurement

In industrial situations, the ability to inspect and, if necessary, reject quickly is desirable if further errors are to be prevented. The value of microcomputer-controlled inspection equipment lies in moving probes at high speed or using several probes simultaneously, and in analysing the reading obtained to produce a final result quickly and with consistent accuracy. For example, in checking turbine blades, twenty transducers might be used simul-taneously. Immediate indication of 'oversize', 'undersize' or 'acceptable' for each of the twenty measurements is given by lamps (red, orange, green) and a printout is available for permanent record.

The individual readings can be conveniently stored to allow trends, etc. to be identified. This often enables a situation to be altered before faulty work is produced.

For precision engineering an important measurement is surface quality expressed by about twenty parameters (e.g. roundness). The calculation of these parameters is tedious working from a trace of the surface. Traditional surface measurement instruments provide analog output into, say, chart recorders. By interfacing a microcomputer to the output of the instrument, the analysis can be done directly. In this type of application therefore there are microprocessor-based surface measurement instruments and also 'add on' systems.

11.8 A microprocessor application in an analytical laboratory

Often to achieve reasonable labour productivity in a laboratory, the test equipment needs to be automatic in operation without the continuous presence of a tech-nician. The inclusion of microprocessors in some test equipment allows this manner of operation to be realised.

The following section describes one of the micro-processor-based instruments being used in an oil com-pany's laboratories. This instrument is an atomic absorp-tion spectrometer.

Atomic absorption spectrometry is a method for deter-mining the concentration of an element in a sample by measuring the absorption of radiation in atomic vapour. The vapour is produced from the sample at a wavelength that is specific and characteristic of the element under consideration. A schematic diagram of the method is shown in Figure 11.3.

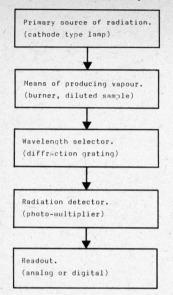

Figure 11.3   Schematic of atomic absorption method

A microprocessor-based absorption spectrometer allows:

1 Automation of spectrometer physical parameters including wavelength, spectral bandwith, lamp turret position, lamp current and data processing conditions;
2 Automation of the atomiser systems including gas flows for the burner and heating program for the graphite furnace;
3 Automation of multi-element sampling devices;
4 Provision for permanent storage and retrieval of analytical programs;
5 Correction for background absorption throughout the entire ultra-violet and visible region.

Control is possible over each specific instrument function, i.e. wavelength, lamp position, etc. The instrument is programmed for each parameter separately by entering the desired value on the keyboard.

Complete programs of analysis can be recalled from memory. If required, the instrument can be triggered by an external device. A block diagram of the system is shown in Figure 11.4.

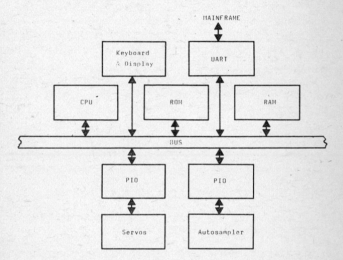

Figure 11.4 Block diagram of absorption spectrometer

All control signals from the microprocessor are based upon spectrometric, instrument status and external command information. The photometric signal is fed periodically to the microprocessor by an A/D converter. Commands from the microprocessor control photomultiplier voltage, spectral slit width, lamp turret position, lamp current and background corrector current. Wavelength is controlled by sending pulses to a motor which fixes the grating position.

The program operates with interrupts at any time in response to external control signals. After each interrupt, for example, to gather photometric data 60 times per second, the program continues from where it left off.

Feedback allows the microprocessor to adjust the instrumentation based upon the current signals received. In this way, for example, optimum electronic gain is achieved.

In use the spectrometer is connected to a mainframe computer. The mainframe is connected to several instrumentation systems and the results from these are stored on a common data base. Reports can be produced as and when required.

The impact of the spectrometer has been to allow 70 samples per hour to be analysed, compared to 6 per hour on the previous system, with a corresponding increase in turn-round time. Estimated labour savings are 60%. Prospective employees are assessed, not as industrial chemists, but on their ability to operate sophisticated machinery. There has been standardisation of analytical procedures, the analytical chemist specifying the software requirements.

12 Transport Applications

12.1 Introduction

Transportation covers land, sea and air systems. From the point of view of discussing microcomputer applications, the transportation system can be regarded as comprising two elements, the signalling and traffic control aspects and the vehicles themselves. This chapter does not cover signalling and traffic control as the systems themselves have not radically changed. Microcomputers allow the systems to be more sophisticated but the principles involve a combination of process control and data communications. The process control is often carried out over such a large geographic area that a data communications system is required to connect the various subsystems. A factor that is always a consideration in transportation systems is safety.

The relatively cheap cost of microcomputers allows additional redundancy to be built into systems when safety is of paramount importance. For example, one railroad signalling system uses three trackside microcomputers. If one becomes faulty, the remaining one(s) shut(s) it down and assume(s) control.

This chapter discusses two common means of transportation, road vehicles and aircraft. The changes, due to microprocessors, in road vehicles are largely related to engine control but other aspects such as gear changing are also being developed.

In contrast to road vehicles, the changes in aircraft systems are less obvious to the passenger, a major area of application being flight management.

12.2   Road vehicle application

Trip indicators and dashboard displays

Modifying conventional dashboard displays using LEDs, fluorescent or liquid crystal displays, to indicate the state of various parts of the system such as engine temperature, brake pressure, outside air temperature are obvious changes that can be made to car instrumentation. A calculating capability as an 'add on' gadget to give trip time, elapse time, average speed, etc. is another simple application.

Cost effective microcomputer applications however arise when the microcomputer is monitoring and controlling the performance of the vehicle. These types of application result in fuel saving or longer component life rather than just enhancing the driver's environment. Thus many of the most fruitful applications will not be so readily obvious to the driver.

Engine control

The design and the settings of controls during operation of an engine require the optimal balance of conflicting specifications, i.e. low fuel consumption versus good acceleration. Applying microcomputers to the job of monitoring current conditions and altering engine controls is a specific case of process control.

One microcomputer control system monitors the following seven parameters:

Barometric pressure;
Carburettor air temperature;
Coolant temperature;
Crankshaft position;
Exhaust gas recirculation (EGR) valve position;
Manifold pressure;
Throttle position.

Signals from these sensors are sent to the control unit mounted in the passenger compartment. The control unit contains the microcomputer, a power supply with a reference voltage for all the sensors, and a masked ROM.

The control unit computes three parameters:

Correct ignition timing;
EGR flowrate;
Airflow rate;

and sends the appropriate commands to the ignition unit, EGR solenoid, and airflow solenoid.

Signals from the sensors are analysed, actual and desired valve positions are compared, and adjustments are made at about 20 times a second.

Transmission controller

Gear changing is another area in which there is a need to analyse several conditions and act accordingly.

A microprocessor-based gear box controller has been developed to be a plug-in replacement on existing vehicles, i.e. to fit into the space currently available. The specification was to develop a 5-speed gear box having a manual hold in some gears.

The parameters monitored and input to the controller are:

Occurrence of 'kick down';
Gear select;
Road speed;
Pressure of air lines;
Gear in use.

From this information, the controller actuates the appropriate gear selection mechanism. As the selection of the gear depends upon the software, variable gearbox characteristics are possible. That is, the controller can operate as a 'close ratio' box or normal as required, the gearbox hardware remaining the same.

Other features are that reverse gear cannot be engaged unless the forward speed is less than 5 mph. The failsafe condition is 5th gear so that the vehicle does not become immobilised, but can be driven 'home'.

Further developments in microprocessor applications are electronically controlled solenoids to replace cam shafts, tappet and con-rods. The need to consider the microprocessor from the original design stage, as opposed to it being an 'add on' system, will lead to changes in the basic design of several other car parts; for example, the design of carburettors could be quite different.

Electric harness

A typical car has approximately thirty bundles of wiring harnesses, each consisting of wires cut to exact length. This system is amenable to a bus system. One harness supplier has developed a co-axial cable bus. The advantage of using co-axial as opposed to flat wire is that the surface area of the outer conductor is much larger than the inner core. Thus the outer co-axial sheath carries the heavy current and the inner cable the control information. In this application, for example, the horn would be activated by a particular pattern of bits on the control/address bus. Furthermore, information could be relayed back along the control bus indicating, for example, that a particular light had failed.

Given that, with normal production volumes, the cost of the system would be comparable to conventional harness systems, the advantages come from less body weight (and hence less fuel consumption) and greater reliability. (One manufacturer sets aside twice the cost of the harness per car to cover warranty claims due to faulty wiring.)

Vehicle communication

Apart from normal voice communication between a driver and his base over a radio link, microprocessor-based equipment is available that will send automatic signals. The possible use of this is to combat hijacking and to provide information in the event of an accident.

In the event of hijacking, an automatic alarm could be transmitted to base. If accidents occur, police or rescue agencies with reception equipment could be immediately informed of the goods being carried, special fire hazards, etc.

Apart from sending automatic signals as outlined above, such a system could have an ASCII keyboard and VDU incorporated.

12.3   Air transport

The sophistication and high hourly cost of operating aircraft make them a natural user of microcomputer systems. Large aircraft can obtain benefits from a distributed processing approach, that is, instead of one central on-board computer, dedicated microcomputer systems can be assigned to each control system and interconnected via a simple bus system. Apart from any operating efficiencies, the saving in cable runs (and hence weight) can justify this approach.

Small aircraft having smaller crews can obtain many benefits from the analysing capability of a microprocessor-based navigation system. The extreme example of this being single seater fighter aircraft.

Commercial airlines can utilise microcomputer systems in many facets of their operations. Three are described here: passenger handling, flight management and maintenance of computer systems.

Passenger handling

One major airline is using microcomputers to control the embarkation of airline passengers through turnstiles. At the check-in gate a boarding pass is produced by a special printer. The boarding pass is printed with details of the journey in 'plain language' for the passenger and also in encoded information which can be read automatically by the barriers at the gate lounge.

A computer maintains a record of the number of boarding passes issued and provides a constant picture of information relating to passenger flow in real-time.

It is intended to extend the passenger system further by introducing credit cards that can be used in a similar manner to cash point machines to issue passengers with their tickets.

Previously passengers completed a boarding card in the departure lounge. When the flight was called, those who arrived at the plane first obtained seats. This system caused confusion and rushes to the plane. In some cases, passengers did not obtain seats even though they had arrived early in the departure lounge.

The new system gives passengers their own individual flight numbers. When the plane is to depart only the relevant numbers are called. The 'ticket' acts as a seat reservation system. On internal flights, the passenger pays on the aircraft. Previously, the passengers bought their tickets prior to entering the departure lounge.

Although the control of passengers will be smoother, some passengers may not like the loss of a more personal system.

Flight management

Microcomputer-aided flight management can make substantial improvements to fuel economy. Normally, fuel economy is dependent upon the attentiveness of the flight crew and their ability to determine an optimum flight path. For example, starting the engines one minute later prior to taxi-ing would save tens of thousands of pounds per year on a major aircraft fleet. Similar savings can be made by reducing the taxi-ing time. Operating within a small margin of optimum altitude can save trip fuel; this can amount to several million pounds a year for major airlines. Cruising marginally faster than optimum uses more fuel. If the aircraft is retrimmed in flight to compensate for changes in centre of gravity further fuel savings are made. Several million pounds may be wasted through inappropriate descent rates. To assist in these and other aspects of flight management, several airlines are using a performance data computer system.

This type of system interfaces with sensors which measure atmospheric conditions and aircraft characteristics and computes the optimum flight profile for best operating costs. There are four sensor inputs: temperature of outside air, altitude, air speed, fuel weight. The pilot inputs 'dispatch data' into the computer prior to take off. This information includes outside air temperature, height of airport at destination, quantity of reserve fuel and fuel for nearest alternative airport, weight of aircraft (including payload less fuel), a given index indicating relationship between fuel cost and time cost.

Once the dispatch data has been entered, the crew can, during the preflight phase, assess the effect of changing the flight plan received. This may be necessary and/or worthwhile because flight plans are based upon meteorological information and traffic conditions that are perhaps four hours old.

The severest operational use of aircraft engines occurs during takeoff. This use of the engines, although of only a short duration, is the single largest contributor to the degradation of the engine performance. The computer system provides for three modes of operation and appropriate parameters can be selected and engaged by the pilot.

During climb the crew traditionally have a choice of two schedules – fast or slow. With the flight management system four modes are offered:

Economy climb;
Maximum rate;
Constant rate;
Thrust target.

In each case, with the sensors monitoring the prevailing conditions the optimum climb profile is followed.

During the flight, whenever the altitude departs from the optimum, this fact is displayed to the crew. Predictions of current range, in distance and time, are displayed. The crew can enter alternative wind speeds, etc. and be given predictions of the effects of these changes. This type of information, which can be required very rapidly if an engine has to be shut down, can also be analysed further by the flight management system to indicate alternative modes of operation to achieve, for example, greatest cruising range under an 'engine out' condition.

Failures within the airborne computer system itself will be stored in memory to be interrogated by the maintenance force on landing.

Microprocessor-based maintenance systems

Workshop rectification methods are different for computer systems. Traditionally, the technician would use a test set to simulate the faulty conditions and follow the signal path to isolate the faulty component.

A microprocessor-based test set, however, will go through a test routine automatically. The fault will be displayed on the test set and the technician then removes the indicated faulty module. This module is then interfaced with another test set enabling the technician to identify the faulty component.

With this approach it is unnecessary for the technician to understand the troubleshooting process. He will need to be trained in the use of the test sets, the effectiveness of the rectification process being dependent upon the designer of the system.

13 Leisure and Consumer Industry Applications

13.1 Introduction

Many products and systems used by the public incorporate microprocessors. Within the home the applications are largely in specific products. Outside the home the facilities provided by familiar products have been enhanced.

Domestic products requiring flexibility in their operation are ideal applications for microprocessors. Thus electronic washing machines can offer a wider range of wash cycles and at the same time become more reliable, as a result of replacing timing motors and cams. In a similar way, a greater variety of facilities can be designed into a micro-processor-controlled sewing machine.

The domestic cooker can normally only be preset to a single temperature. A programmable cooker allows a more extensive cooking program, for example, the oven when it comes on, can go to a very high temperature for say 15 minutes to 'seal' meat and then reduce automatically to the normal roasting temperature.

It is claimed that electronic thermostats have a much smaller hysterisis than electromechanical ones. The benefit in changing to electronic control is that excessive temperature cycling is avoided and fuel bills reduced.

Microelectronics have been used in a variety of electronic games which are linked to television sets, to provide video displays. In many of these, the games selection is in the form of a plug-in cartridge containing either a cassette for loading into a RAM or the cartridge contains a ROM as a plug-in module.

Outside the home, the consumer is likely to meet the effect of microprocessors in many aspects of retailing, i.e. supermarkets, banks, garages, etc. In addition to the technology and techniques discussed in earlier chapters, the consumer is coming into contact with bar code markings on products and using plastic bank/authorisation cards on an ever-increasing scale.

This chapter discusses these two techniques and also covers developments in coin-operated machines. Finally, a short account of one aspect of changes behind the scene in the entertainment business is given – the computer control of stage lighting.

13.2   Retailing and point-of-sale terminals

The point-of-sale terminal has developed from the efforts to simplify the procedures resulting from a sale at a cash register. The initial function of a cash register was to register a sale to the satisfaction of the customer and to ensure that, as far as possible, the till held the money securely. To help in the subsequent reconciliation of the takings with the reduction in stock due to sales, tally rolls were produced containing details of the sales made. A copy of the sale 'rung up' could also be produced as a receipt for the customers.

As computer systems developed the linking of cash registers to computers began to be considered. The development of optical character recognition (OCR) led to the printing of the tally rolls using OCR characters. The tally roll could then be input to a computer system for analysis.

The development of on-line computer systems led to the cash register being considered as a computer terminal, the output from the terminal going directly into a computer or alternatively being recorded on magnetic tape cassettes. Once the concept of having the sales takings analysed by a computer has been established attention was directed to more sophisticated ways of inputting sales information to the point-of-sale terminal (POS).

In addition to keyboard input, the POS terminal is usually equipped with an optical symbol pen reader or magnetic stripe pen reader. The products to be sold are marked with their product code and when sold this mark is read automatically by using a suitable pen at the POS. In this way more detailed information can be passed to the computer system allowing a more elaborate analysis of sales, stock turnover rates, etc. A block diagram of a microprocessor controlled POS terminal is shown in Figure 13.1. The ROM typically contains the decoding instructions

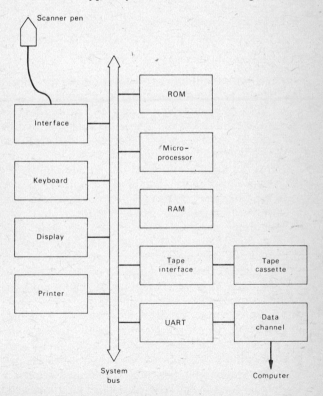

Figure 13.1 Block diagram of a point-of-sale terminal

to suit the scanning system used. The tape cassette unit allows a record of the day's activities to be stored for subsequent updating of the central computer's files for a POS that is not on-line. Prices and similar information may also be input into the RAM from tape or from the central computer.

The optical system used in supermarkets on food products, etc. consists of bar marking. Allocation of the codes to be used are controlled by national agencies. The codes in many cases are incorporated in the packaging design of the product.

At the checkout when the product is scanned, the computer system identifies the product and recalls the current price from memory. These prices can take into account discounts or special offers. The customer can be given a printed itemised list of purchases including brief alphabetic descriptions of the items instead of just the price.

13.3   Bar coding

Bar coding on retail products conforms to one of two similar systems, the European Article Number system (EAN) or the Universal Product Code (UPC). The EAN system has thirteen digits and the UPC twelve digits. The Article Numbering Association in the United Kingdom have ensured that the EAN code is substantially compatible to the UPC as established in the United States and Canada.

The first digit in the UPC system and the first two digits in the EAN system indicate the country that issued the number. The next ten digits are structured according to the standard of the issuing country. Usually, the first four or five of these digits comprise the code issued by the appropriate country's numbering association to identify the manufacturer. The second five or six digits are allocated by the manufacturer to code the product.

Each variation of the product has to be allocated a unique code. Therefore, different codes are required for variations in packaging, weight, colour, etc. The final digit is a check digit to ensure that the bar scanner has read the code correctly.

Each digit or character position consists of seven bar positions. A dark bar represents a 1 bit, a light bar a 0 bit. When read the code is usually interpreted from look-up tables in ROM.

In use a pen may be passed over a label in either direction depending upon the orientation of the product at a checkout point. To enable the system to read the code correctly under these conditions, it is necessary for the system to be able to deduce the direction of pen scan. This is achieved by the lefthand character codes having odd parity and the righthand characters even parity. Two codes therefore exist for each character in the look-up tables previously mentioned.

To synchronise the codes being read by the pen correctly the label has additional bar patterns. The lefthand margin of the label is at least eleven bars wide and the first marks encountered are three bits, 101 (guard bars). The centre of the label has a standard 5-bit bar (01010). At the right-hand side of the bar code is a further guard bar of 101. The right-hand margin is a minimum of seven bars wide.

It is customary to print human readable characters along the bottom edge of the bar code in optical character font (OCR-B).

13.4 Portable data capture

The restocking of goods in retailing operations can involve a great deal of paperwork. As the size and cost of data capture devices have fallen, the move is towards taking the data capture device to the place where the restocking decision is made rather than sending paperwork to a centralised system.

A portable data capture device consists of a handheld keyboard, similar to a pocket calculator. Information keyed in may be retained in non-volatile memory or recorded onto a portable tape cassette. Non-volatile memory allows the data capture unit to be switched off without loss of the contents of the memory.

In a store or supermarket, the data capture device may also include a handheld bar code scanner (wand). Bar codes of each product line are displayed on the shelves. Re-ordering consists of touring the shelves passing the wand over any item code to be re-ordered. The quantity to be re-ordered may be entered via the keyboard or may be a standard quantity held on the computer files. For unusual and extra large orders the standard quantity can be ordered several times by several passes of the wand.

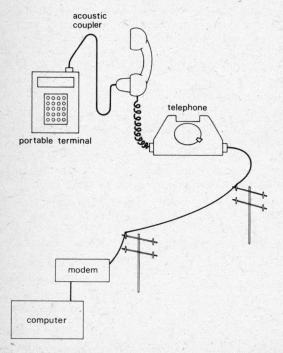

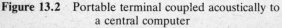

Figure 13.2   Portable terminal coupled acoustically to a central computer

Portable data entry terminals can be used by sales representatives to take orders during the day. In the evening, the salesman connects the portable terminal to his home telephone via a plug-in acoustic coupler and transmits his orders to the company's central computer (see Figure 13.2). The most elaborate of these systems allows the central computer to transmit back acknowledgement of orders and give details of credit limits, special offers, etc. for the next day's calls. This information is extracted from the terminal by the salesman in the morning before setting off on his calls.

As these portable data terminals are microprocessor-based, the facilities and sophistication varies amongst the different makes. Some terminals, being programmable, have the appropriate program downloaded from the central computer as required. The rate of transference over the public telephone system is 2400 bauds. Alternatively, local loading of programs is done by pluggable modules containing EPROMs.

The first section of terminal memory is semi-permanent and contains the salesman's user code. Bulk transmission of the terminal's memory therefore will always be proceeded by suitable identification codes. Changing this code requires a different keying sequence to that used to edit the rest of the information in the memory.

The pocket terminal is internally powered by rechargeable batteries and can be recharged either from the mains or from a car's cigarette lighter socket.

13.5 Badge readers and other data capture devices

A card reader is a type of data capture device that is being employed increasingly to authorise the use of unattended equipment or facilities.

The card carries coded data on a magnetic stripe. When the user inserts the card into the reader, use of the system is authorised or denied according to the code presented.

Typical applications for card readers include access

control to restricted areas, such as research laboratories or car parks, and access to the use of equipment such as VDUs or photocopiers. A further use is as authorisation to carry out banking transactions at a banking terminal.

The interrogation system used in conjunction with badge readers can be programmed to suit many circumstances. Time zones can be established allowing access only during predetermined hours. This aspect may be developed further to monitor and control the times when security guards report via terminal devices on their tours. The equipment can also incorporate anti-passback features to avoid more than one person using the same card by passing it back from one person to another.

Badge card readers used as access control devices are connected to a central controller. This central controller may be a dedicated piece of microprocessor equipment rather than part of a general computer system. The central controller is linked to the badge readers via a common two wire circuit, usually co-axial cable. One such system allows the wire to be up to 5 miles long. Additional readers are connected into the system by tapping the wires with a connection box, see Figure 13.3. A typical central controller can have up to 120 card readers connected and handle over 60,000 card holders. In addition to monitoring the use of cards, the controller can monitor up to four environmental alarms from each card reader station. Self-contained power supplies enable the controller to function for 48 hours in the event of a mains power failure.

It is possible to change the void/valid status of a card immediately at the control unit. If necessary, a printer can be incorporated in the system to provide a record of movement through the card controlled barriers.

Badge card readers can be the basis of more elaborate data entry equipment that include a keyboard to enter unique data and a printer to output responses from the central control unit or computer.

This type of unit is used by banks to allow customers to

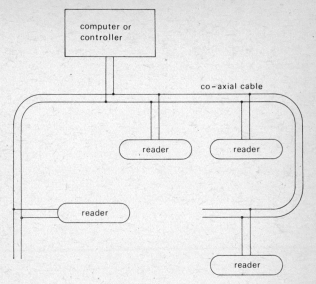

Figure 13.3 Data link for remote data capture devices

withdraw money, pay in money or request statements, etc.

13.6 Electronic coin mechanisms

The proliferation of coin-operated machines around the world has led to manufacturers seeking ways to standardise the coin mechanism. Various qualities of mechanism are available, the low price type being used where the economic consequences of abuse or fraud does not justify a sophisticated mechanism. The higher quality mechanism is gradually being standardised dimensionally as 5 inches wide, 15 inches deep and 3 inches wide.

Standardising the mechanism to cope with all types of coinage requires more complex electronic circuits. Three inductive sensors are used to detect coin diameter, thickness and metal content. The necessity to give change, in the three lowest coin values using the minimum of coins, has caused one manufacturer to incorporate an opto-electronic sensor system on the coin tubes.

The change from mechanical relays to electronic methods has resulted in much faster switching speeds, so that coin bounce routines have to be incorporated in the software.

A specification for a coin mechanism developed by one major manufacturer covers the following aspects:

Up to four different coins can be accepted between a range of diameters; there is an inductive tuning capability which rejects most 'foreign' coins;

Change is given using a minimum number of coins lying within a range of diameters;

There is an indication if change is unavailable;

The operative price range can be adjusted in a series of steps to suit the lowest coin required;

Four different prices may be set on the mechanism at the same time;

There are facilities to return coins under specified circumstances as determined by the program logic.

The need to adapt the coin mechanism to different coin currencies is met by setting binary switches. This allows a mechanism to be converted from one currency to another by a simple re-setting up procedure whereas previously the mechanisms were tailor-made for individual countries.

Vending machine

The use of this type of mechanism in a vending machine is described below.

As coins are inserted by the user the total entered is displayed as credit. When an item is selected the micro-processor controller checks if the item is available. If so, three further checks are made, is the credit sufficient? is there sufficient change available? can the exact change be given? The user can insert further coins and select additional items according to his credit, or request his change.

When change is requested coins are dispensed, beginning with the highest denomination, until either that coinage runs out or the remaining credit is less than the value of that coin. The process is then repeated on the next lower coin denomination.

In one particular system, the software is kept as compact as possible by avoiding interrupts. The various inputs are scanned in turn to give a stable loop condition. This is broken by a customer starting the previously described chain of events by inserting a coin.

Juke boxes

The modern juke box is a microprocessor-based system whereby control of the record playing unit is from remotely mounted coin-operated wallboxes. There may be several wallboxes connected to a common record unit. A block diagram of a microprocessor-based wallbox is shown in Figure 13.4.

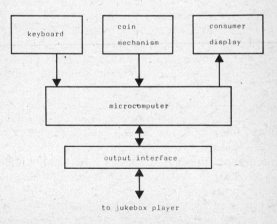

Figure 13.4 Juke box wallbox control

The wallbox unit contains a coin mechanism as previously described to provide customer credit. In addition, there is a keyboard allowing the entry of 3-digit numbers (0 to 999) and a reset key. The customer display indicates the credit status and the selection made.

Push button payphones

The Post Office has developed a microprocessor coin-operated 'phone. When coins are inserted the total is displayed. As a call proceeds the amount displayed diminishes according to the charge rate applicable to the coded 'phone number dialled. Ten seconds before the credit expires a warning light is activated. At the end of a call the machine will return unspent coins. It does not give change but simply returns unspent coins.

Since payphones are connected to a telecommunications network, any fault that develops in the operation of the payphone can be signalled to alert repair staff.

13.7   Garage forecourt sales

The monitoring of the sales of petrol at petrol pumps and the display of the quantity and cost at a kiosk control unit is a natural application of microprocessor control.

There are several systems in use but they are all based upon similar principles. When the customer concludes his use of a pump, the pump number and cost is displayed or printed in the kiosk. With a VDU, the display entry can be cancelled via the keyboard after payment. The hardcopy from a printer may act as a receipt or the kiosk attendant crosses off the printed bill as it is paid.

Apart from any customer convenience, the value of the system to the garage comes from the analysis of the cumulative sales. At the end of each day, a total sales printout may be obtained by pump, by grade of fuel, and the remaining stocks in each storage tank notified. A garage using this system in a suburban area found that the duties of a full-time clerk could be reduced to half an hour.

13.8 Stage lighting

The main function of lighting control systems are to provide a central control point and to allow the brightness of each light to be controlled. Traditionally, the brightness is controlled manually by means of dimmer switches.

The contribution microcomputer systems can make to stage lighting control is to provide a memory feature. The advantages gained by a computer controlled system can best be appreciated by considering the features of a typical system.

The lighting channels can be selected from a single keyboard. This keyboard is also used for re-programming. The lighting channels called up can have their lighting level altered and the speed of change can be specified. A series of cues across all the lights can be set up. Lamps that require a longer warm-up time will be 'brought in' in a different manner from the rest.

The lighting 'patterns' and cues when recorded can be edited, and additional cues inserted. In this way, a programme of lighting effects can be built up.

In use the current state of the channels are displayed on a VDU together with details of the next cue. Touching a GO button initiates the next cue. If necessary all or parts of the control sequence can be overridden manually.

The system is of assistance when a stage production is being planned. The lighting manager can call up 'enblock' pre-recorded effects and patterns, whereas previously every single light had to be altered manually. Thus the lighting manager can 'design' his production more effectively and quickly.

The recorded cues allow rehearsals to proceed more smoothly than with a manual system, since with the latter it was difficult to back-track to some previous lighting position.

From an ergonomic aspect, the computer-controlled system can produce cues in rapid succession, which just could not be implemented in the time available by a manual system.

14 Educational Applications

14.1 Introduction

This chapter discusses some developments and gives examples of applications that are predominantly educational.

The ability to make television sets more 'intelligent' at little additional cost has laid the foundation to a new way of disseminating knowledge and information on a wider scale than ever before. Some see the development of videotex as the most significant development in information dissemination since the invention of printing. It has also given rise to the concept of the 'information provider'. These developments are covered in the first part of this chapter.

Coupled with the possibilities of videotex, the low cost of microcomputers has given a greater momentum to educational establishments to develop computer assisted learning (CAL) material. A simple example of a computer-assisted instruction program is described in this chapter.

The special requirements of CAL have led to the development of further higher level languages. An outline of one, PILOT, is given together with a portion of a Tiny PILOT program.

To illustrate the possibilities of using the hardware itself (microprocessors and microcomputers) a microcomputer control and reporting project is described. This project (introduced in chapter 8, section 8.4) brought together computer, engineering and management (user) personnel who all gained knowledge and experience from the project.

14.2   Videotex

Videotex is the general term for the transmission of digitally encoded frames which can be received and displayed on modified television sets. There are two transmission systems, which broadcast over TV channels or over a public telephone network.

Broadcast videotex is also known as Teletext and is a one-way, non-interactive system. The transmission of frames over a telephone network allows interactive use and is termed Interactive Videotex (initially it was called Viewdata). There are various services available using these systems that have proprietary names, e.g.

Broadcast based systems, *Ceefax*, *Oracle*, etc.
Interactive based systems, *Prestel*, *Telidon*, etc.

A frame of videotex consists of twenty-four lines of forty characters. A 'page' is the unit of information accessed by the user and may consist of up to twenty-six frames. For example, page 321 may consist of three frames, 321a, 321b, 321c.

The structure of the database and page numbering allows each page to lead to up to ten subsidiary lower level pages (known as filials). The filial's number is added to the higher level page number as a least significant figure, i.e. page 1 leads to pages 10, 11, 12, etc. page 11 leads to 110, 111, etc.

The systems have a colour capability based on the three fundamental colours (red, green, blue) being on or off in any combination. This provides eight colours, red, green, yellow, blue, magenta, cyan, black and white.

The encoded transmission also allows double height characters and on/off flashing of sections of the frame.

Broadcast videotex

This is a non-interactive system because the broadcasting company repeatedly transmits an entire set of frames.

When the user specifies the page on his control unit, the receiver selects, stores and displays the page when it next comes round.

The encoded frames are transmitted as the first lines of the normal TV broadcast picture. (These first lines are not seen on a correctly adjusted TV set.) It takes approximately a quarter of a second to transmit a frame and a user would wait on average 20 seconds if the service consisted of 100 frames. This reflects one of the limitations of broadcast videotex, only about 100–200 frames can be contemplated if the waiting time is to be realistic, whereas interactive videotex can offer ¼–½ million frames, say, without this restriction.

Limitations on the practical number of frames that can be offered on TV channels have led to other possibilities being considered. If every line of the screen could be used for digital transmissions instead of the top few out of sight of the picture, approximately 15,000 frames could be offered to the user without increasing the waiting time. This leads to the idea of offering specialised services at night after normal broadcasing hours or the use of dedicated TV channels.

Interactive videotex

The transmission of videotex over public telephone networks requires the modified TV set to be connected via a modem and adaptor to the telephone. The modem converts the digital signal to analog and vice-versa, as explained in chapter 9. The adaptor consists of a memory for storing the signal and a character generator. Signals to the TV set also need to have the correct scanning and synchronisation elements added. In addition, the user has a keypad consisting of twelve keys, 0 to 9, * and #.

A TV set with the above modifications could connect to a videotex system automatically. On the user initiating the connection, the computer would be dialled up automatically. After the ringing tone the computer would send a 1,300 Hz tone indicating it was answering. The user number and password would then be entered manually, or automatially if required. Once connected the user is presented with the main menu.

Apart from working downwards through the tree-like structure of the pages, keying special combinations such as * *n* # takes the user direct to page *n* and * # takes the user back to the previous page viewed.

The interactive nature of these systems allows the user to respond to instructions and options displayed on the screen. For example, a user could request a brochure from an advertiser.

Information providers

The owner of the videotex system sells pages to information providers (IPs). Charges for accessing pages are decided by the information provider and vary from nothing for advertisements to top rates for specialised information such as stock market data.

The information provider is similar to a publisher and may take a block of pages to re-let in smaller quantities. Typical information providers using viewdata systems include:

Newspapers;
Magazine publishers;
Banks and credit card companies;
Commercial firms, providing the stocking situation of their products;
Travel organisations, providing timetables;
Encyclopaedia publishers.

The basis of charging and accessing information may be controlled at the receiving end. For example, in hotels certain information may be obtainable 'free' as part of the service, other pages may include a charge for use of the equipment. Some services may require passwords before the pages can be accessed, such as for the legal and medical professions.

Telesoftware

The more sophisticated user may want to access information, store it and manipulate it locally. There is thus a need for interfacing the videotex system with a microcomputer. This would allow, for example, stock prices to be monitored via the videotex and personalised graphs and charts to be displayed. The imaginative use of the information provided could well be beyond the expectation of the information provider.

However, having an 'intelligent' terminal connected into the videotex systems leads to a further service, telesoftware. Information providers could provide software that is downloaded into the user's terminal. Also the terminal could act as a remote data entry station.

The availability of encyclopaedia matter via videotex and the ability to download common software to many establishments is likely to have a considerable effect on educational methods and technologies.

14.3 Computer assisted learning

As computers have developed, become more widely available and simpler to use, more attention has been devoted to using computers to assist in the learning process. The development of microprocessors and hence microcomputers is a significant event in computer assisted learning for two reasons:

1 The devices are now considerably cheaper than mainframes and within the budgets of many more schools and colleges;
2 Microcomputers are small and portable, allowing convenient hands-on experience in almost any situation.

For these reasons, there has been an explosion of computer applications to learning situations in schools, colleges and training etablishments. So much so that there are many groups trying to co-ordinate and disseminate details of the on-going activities, e.g. The Council for Educational Technology for the United Kingdom (CET), Microcomputer Users in Schools and Education (MUSE).

The role of computers in education can be classified under several aspects:

1 The computer can present a user with a series of problems or tests and score the responses. Because of its interactive nature the sequence of tests can be made dependent upon the answers. Thus weak areas can be re-inforced by further testing and practice.

2 The computer can be used as a direct extension of programmed learning, but with greater flexibility in presenting the information to be learned.

3 The computer can be used to model and simulate almost any situation. Thus medical students can simulate operations without any untoward effects if the 'patient' dies. Prior to the wider use of computers more expensive and less flexible analog models were used.

4 The computer can be the provider of information and the analyser of data for specific topics of study. Thus a suitable database will allow students to engage in, say, more realistic demographic projects and research as part of their geography and statistics studies.

5 The computer can maintain records relating to the progress of students to be used in a computer-managed learning (CML) context.

The use of computers in education affects the learning situation in a number of ways. The teaching is more individual and can be self-paced. In some cases, the impersonal aspects of using a computer can be an advantage. Not everyone is willing to disclose to another person their lack of understanding, or fears. It has been found, for example, that many patients are much more forthcoming in responding to a 'questionnaire' on a computer than in discussing their symptoms with a doctor.

Using a computer for instruction or learning allows the participants to start at any time; there is no need to wait for or schedule a group. This represents a radical change from traditional teaching and training methods whereby groups are assembled for teaching purposes.

The extent to which these features modify an organisation's approach to its teaching or training activities depends upon their nature. The portability of microcomputers will result in the scope of these activities to be increased.

Computer-aided instruction (CAI) is sometimes distinguished from computer-assisted learning (CAL), to reflect the difference between training (CAI) and education (CAL). An area of application that lends itself to computer assistance is fault analysis. In the example that is described below it will be regarded as CAI.

Traditionally, fault analysis is carried out by means of check lists of possible faults together with associated symptoms. If necessary, the cause and effect relationships are explained and the remedial action to be taken given. The procedure can be made more systematic, and unnecessary testing reduced, by presenting the procedure as a logic tree (similar to a computer flowchart). Logic trees can spread over many pages and, because of the limited space available within the symbols for annotation, still require extensive back-up reference material.

CAI allows the 'complexity' of the logic tree to be built into the program thereby shielding the user from this feature. Using a computer also allows the relevant back-up material to be presented to the user immediately as required, as screen instruction, explanations or diagrams.

The degree to which the user learns or remembers the procedure might be incidental. Even an 'expert' might be expected to follow the program so that no aspect is omitted by oversight.

If the intention is to have the user learn the procedure and eventually become independent of the program, then a further program could be written that tests for an understanding of the procedure. This allows training officers to release to departments only those who have reached a required proficiency. For more complex procedures, test results allow a learning curve to be constructed for individuals identifying those who will never attain the proficiency required.

14.4   An example of CAI fault analysis

The example to be described was developed as a demonstration of CAI principles for use in Training Officer and Personnel Management courses. The test to be undertaken, under computer-directed instructions, is the detection and rectification of faults in an appliance mains plug.

The first routine instructs the user to switch off and unplug the appliance and then remove the top. Explanations and guidance are then given as to the correct wiring. If the user responds 'Yes' to the question, 'Is the wiring correct?' the program continues to the next stage. If the response is 'No', the user is asked to remove and refit wires as indicated on the screen.

The second stage of the program then alternately explains and questions the user on a series of possible faults, related to the condition of the connections within the plug, e.g. damage, stray or loose strands. Each time the user indicates a particular fault is present, instructions are given to correct the defect. Because any work undertaken on the plug could invalidate previous responses, the program logic repeats all the questions after any rectification.

The third stage is entered after all aspects of the wiring is satisfactory. This stage questions the user on the correctness and acceptability of the anchorage of the sheathed cable to the plug.

Finally, a series of explanations and questions are asked

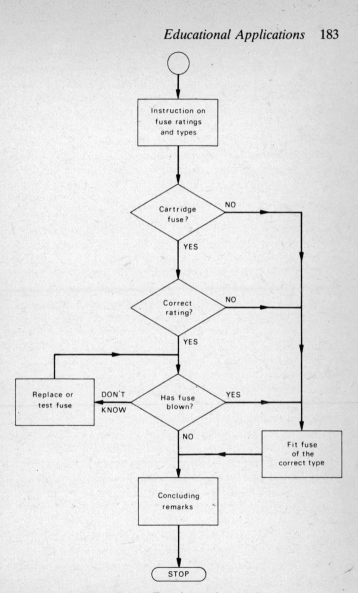

Figure 14.1   Fuse inspection routine

about the fuse. A flow chart of the fuse inspection routine is shown in Figure 14.1. An example of the screen display at the second decision symbol (Is it the correct rating?) is shown in Table 14.1.

```
        FAULT ANALYSIS OF 13 AMP PLUG
        -----------------------------

        CHECKING : FUSE
        --------

   THE FUSE MUST BE OF THE CORRECT RATING
   DEPENDENT UPON THE LOAD (IN WATTS) OF
   THE DEVICE CONNECTED.

      LOADS UP TO        USE FUSE RATED AT
      -----------        -----------------
       500 WATTS             2 AMPS
      1250 WATTS             5 AMPS
      3250 WATTS            13 AMPS
      OVER 3250             SEEK ADVICE
   ----------------------------------------
   IS YOUR FUSE THE CORRECT RATING FOR THE
   APPLICATION, Y/N ?
```

Table 14.1   Screen display at a decision point

This example illustrates how the emphasis in this type of application of CAI is on ensuring that a strict procedure is followed regardless of the user's assumed knowledge.

The example just described could be written in almost any computer language. Interest in applying computers specifically to education and learning has led to the development of special languages. The next section outlines one such language, PILOT.

14.5 PILOT

PILOT is a computer language specifically developed for
CAL use. Teachers and trainers in subjects other than
mathematics and science need to be able to develop
material without acquiring computing and programming
expertise. Also in these other subjects, one does not want
to make students respond in a particular format. As far as
possible if a computer is to be used, the responses should
be as natural as possible.

PILOT is one example of languages that have been
developed with the above two criteria in mind, non-
programmers developing the material and the facility for a
wide range of natural responses from the user. Languages
of this type are sometimes referred to as 'author languages'.

There are several versions of PILOT implemented on a
range of computers. The example described below is
based upon a version as implemented on the PET microcomputer.

Before describing a portion of the program, a brief
comment on the structure of the language is required. The
line numbers in PILOT are often created automatically.
Each line (instruction) consists of an operation code
followed by an optional conditional modifier, a semi-colon
(in this version), and a test field.

The four main operation codes are:

T; text	Any text following the semi-colon is displayed.
A;	Accepts input from the user and stores it in an answer buffer.
M; text	Matches the text following the semi-colon against sub-strings from the contents of the answer buffer.
J; label name	Takes program control to a label corresponding to label name.

Conditional modifiers are usually Y (for a successful
match) and N (for a mis-match). An extract from a PILOT
program is given in Table 14.2.

```
11 *Q2
12 T;WHAT IS THE NAME OF THE LAW THAT
13 T;RELATES VOLTAGE TO CURRENT AND
14 T;RESISTANCE IN THE FOLLOWING
15 T;RELATIONSHIP.  V = I * R
16 T;
17 A;
18 T;
19 M;GIVE UP
20 TY;OHM'S LAW
21 JY;*Q3
22 M;OHM
23 TN;NO. TRY AGAIN. THE LAW IS ASSOCIATED
24 TN;WITH THE NAME OF A PERSON.
25 TN;
26 JN;*Q2
27 M;OHM'S LAW
28 TN;ALMOST RIGHT. AS IT IS NAMED AFTER
29 TN;A PERSON IT IS OHM'S LAW.
30 TY;CORRECT.
31 *Q3
```

Table 14.2 Extract from a program in Tiny PILOT

Line 11 consists of a label (which must start with an ∗). Lines 12 to 15 print the text of a question and line 16 prints a blank line. The user's answer is taken in at line 17 and stored in the answer buffer. Line 22 consists of all or part of a response that is correct or nearly correct. In this case if any part of the user's response contained the string 'OHM' there is a successful match. The text in lines 23 to 25 will be printed if the match is unsuccessful, and in addition line 26 instructs the program control to jump to label ∗Q2. This causes the question to be repeated. If the user did not know the answer or cannot guess it he would be trapped in this endless loop. Lines 19 to 21 allow the user to 'give up'. When the user's response at line 17 is 'GIVE UP' a match occurs at line 19 and the answer (line 20) is printed. A jump is then made to label ∗Q3.

If the user's response contains 'OHM' as a sub-string, thereby giving a match at line 22, then lines 23 to 26 will not be executed. Line 27 is intended to distinguish between the correct answer (OHM'S LAW) and the almost correct answers. These might be 'OHM LAW', 'OHMS RULE' etc. In the case of a correct answer line 30 is executed, otherwise lines 28 and 29 are printed.

This example illustrates the ease with which text can be handled. More elaborate versions of PILOT give greater flexibility, particularly with the match operation code. For example, Common PILOT allows mis-spellings to be anticipated in two ways. If it is felt that an individual letter may be incorrect, the match text can contain an asterisk, e.g.

M; COMPUT*R

This would allow the user to respond with 'COMPUTER', 'COMPUTOR', or 'COMPUTUR' and still obtain a match. When a response may have some of the letters 'correct' but several wrong, & can be used, e.g.

M; SO&C&ER

This anticipates that the correct response, SORCERER, may be mis-spelt. The ampersand allows any number of incorrect letters between the specified text.

PILOT software systems contain a variety of editing features similar to those associated with word processing, i.e. lines can be deleted or inserted, the lines being automatically renumbered. These features are again a consequence of making the development of CAL programs as simple as possible for the non-computer specialist.

The use of author languages, such as PILOT, in CAL are concerned with just one aspect of computer-based learning, whereby the machine (computer) is just another alternative means of acquiring the required knowledge. The development of microprocessors and microcomputers has opened up another avenue of learning, that is the development of hybrid models for experimentation purposes. With expensive mainframes, users could only make use of the systems provided 'at a distance'. A far more adventurous approach can be taken with micros in a hands-on situation. The next section describes a project involving interfacing a 'single-board' microcomputer (the ACORN), a PET microcomputer and an analog model which could not have been considered if only mainframes were available as a 'service' to the user.

14.6 A microcomputer control and reporting system

This section describes a project undertaken by the authors aimed at enabling as many disciplines as possible to co-operate, collaborate and learn from the project as it progressed.

The project involved building an analog model to represent the entities flowing through a system. An ACORN microcomputer controls the workings of the model and a PET microcomputer monitors the operation of the model via the ACORN. Schematic diagrams of the model are given in chapter 8, where system development aspects are described.

Although building a model of balls running down a series of inclines may seem abstract, it allows a number of analogies to be drawn with the model. The flow of balls could be people through baggage handling at an airport, or lorries unloading at depots, or materials flowing through a factory. This last analogy will be the one drawn in describing the project further.

The progress of the balls through the system is determined by the issuing characteristics of the release gate. These are programmable and are under the control of an ACORN microcomputer. Thus a batch of five (say) can be released on to the inclines either at random or at a specified rate. At some juncture in the progress of the balls down the inclines, non-magnetic ones are detected and automatically diverted directly to the final receptacle. Balls that complete the full course are considered as having been completely processed. Further sensing devices can be added to reject balls on the basis of other characteristics.

The project as described so far represents a useful vehicle for experimentation on the use of actuators and sensors and the interfacing of these devices to a microcomputer. It also represents an operating industrial system that needs to be monitored from a management standpoint.

A PET microcomputer is used as a monitoring microcomputer providing 'management' with tables, summaries and graphs of the throughput of the analog model. Using an ACORN to control the model and a PET as a passive monitor provides scope for experimentation on the computing side. There is the opportunity in the interfacing problem to try different approaches to line protocols, interrupts, etc. and to take into account the effect of requiring different response times due to the rate at which signals are coming from the sensors. The project also provides a testbed for developing software that could be put into EPROMs.

Microcomputer reporting

The nature and types of report required will depend on the meaning attached to the analog model. In all cases, however, it is intended that the model is a 'black box'. That is to say, 'management' do not know what is happening at the model except through information obtained from the screen of the PET. For example, if a non-magnetic ball represents a defective item, at the start of a run management will have no knowledge of the numbers defective until the reporting system present the isolated cases. The effectiveness of the management reporting system is judged by its ability to analyse correctly and quickly the true situation. The types of report that are generated on the PET are described below.

1 *On-line report*
This report would be the one normally on display (see Table 14.3). The report shows the time 'production'

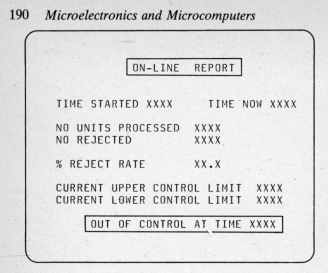

Table 14.3   On-line report from analog model

started and time now. The total number of units (balls) processed, rejected and the percentage reject rate is shown in real time. Based upon a statistical control chart analysis the *current* upper and lower limits are continually being recalculated and displayed.

2   Emergency condition

If the current percentage reject rate goes outside the control limits, a flashing 'out of control' message is added to the display. This message contains the time at which loss of control occurred.

3   Shift report

This report can be displayed on request and provides the following types of information:

Shift no.
Batch size
Batch rate/min
No. started

No. completed
No. rejected
% rejected

At the end of each shift these details are written to a file
and allow the display of the fourth type of report.

4   *Production summary*
The production summary presents a tabulated version of
each shift report together with the total across all shifts.

Value of a project

The model provides a useful test bed across several
disciplines and allows a far more flexible approach to the
simulation of industrial types of system than the normal
dedicated analog model built before the advent of microprocessors.

15 Office Applications

15.1 Introduction

The traditional routines and organisation of office work have been dramatically affected by developments in electronics. This is because much of the equipment used in offices lends itself to being redesigned so as to incorporate microelectronic devices. Additional benefits and degrees of sophistication become possible because electronic devices can be readily interconnected and centrally controlled. The ability to develop co-ordinated systems has led to the 'electronic office'.

The development of the electronic office concept has caused the nature of office work to be re-examined. Traditionally offices are the places where paperwork is processed. Improvements in office routines and efficiency have tended to accept paper as the natural media flowing through and around offices and concentrated on improved methods of handling and storing (filing) paperwork. Paper is however only a means to an end. An office consists of people, paper and files involved in the following activities:

(a)   People to people communication (e.g. telephone);
(b)   People to paper communication (e.g. typing);
(c)   Paper to paper transference (e.g. copying);
(d)   Paper to files (e.g. storing);
(e)   Files to people (e.g. information retrieval).

The essential resource being processed is *information* and the transference process involves *communication*. Thus the essential features of an electronic office, regardless of the media, is to have flexibility of communications and means of storing and retrieving information.

15.2 Word processing

The predominant need in an office is to manipulate textual matter rather than numeric information.

The modern word processor results from combining the developments in computing with the developments in office automation, notably the typewriter.

Manual typewriters are still the norm in the portable field but electric typewriters are commonplace in offices. Developments in electric typewriters, as such, have been mainly associated with the idea of readily changeable typefaces, e.g. the 'golf ball'. In parallel with this, accounting machines had been developed that made use of the idea of storing information on a magnetic strip. The natural extension of this idea is to store general textual material on a magnetic card or disk. The evolution of these 'storage' typewriters has been dramatically enhanced by the coming of the chip.

Traditional computers have always been able to store and manipulate text but at a cost. Hence the development of computer applications has tended to be in the numeric systems of a business, payroll, stock control, etc. The development of the chip has revolutionised the economics of computing text. As microcomputer systems are small, the system can readily be located at the point of use. What cannot be conveniently miniaturised is the input device (a keyboard) and the output device (a printer or screen). However, if one takes an electric typewriter as the basis of a suitable input and output device, there is room to build the complete computer system around the typewriter.

The combining of typewriters with computers, with space no longer a constraint, has led to the development of work stations. That is, to simply build a computer into a typewriter would miss many of the benefits of the concept.

A word processor can be divided into the following functional areas:

(a) Keyboard – the means of input to the system;
(b) Central processor – the computer heart of the system;

(c) Visual display unit (VDU) – a screen for displaying work currently being manipulated via the keyboard;

(d) Disk unit – the unit into which the required files (floppy disks) are slotted by the operator;

(e) Printer – the means of producing 'hard copy' for issue.

Standard letters, address lists, part-written reports, etc. all need to be stored in the word processing system. This type of information (or data) is stored by recording it on to magnetic disks. Any set of information stored on a disk is referred to as a file and is given a filename. The reason for creating files on disks rather than on, say, cassette tapes, is to allow the information to be accessed randomly.

The operator is likely to have a drawer for storing the dozen or so disk files that are used on the system. Because much of the work involves merging of information from two files, e.g. printing names and addresses from one file and printing chosen sections of standard letters from another, the disk unit usually has at least two slots into which floppy disks can be mounted simultaneously.

Use of a word processor

The use of a word processor will be described with respect to producing a standard letter. Initially the operator will type the letter as though using a typewriter. The typed input will be displayed on the screen of the VDU, the current position on the screen being indicated by a flashing cursor symbol.

If the operator makes a mistake, additional keys allow the operator to move the cursor back where required and re-enter the correct version. This automatically overwrites the previous entries. In this way an error-free original is produced prior to printing.

At this stage the letter can be 'saved' on a disk file for subsequent use. The letter can be edited at any time, that is immediately it has been entered or when it has been recalled from a disk. The facilities for editing usually allow a paragraph, a line or a word to be deleted, inserted or changed. This is achieved by specifying the position in the text where the change is to be made, the nature of the change, and if necessary the revised text.

A further facility that might be available is the ability to substitute a word or phrase throughout the entire text wherever it occurs. Thus a standard letter relating to pay changes might contain phrases specifying July as the first month for implementing the changes. If revision of the time scales becomes necessary, a simple instruction by the word processor operator can cause every 'July' in the text to be automatically replaced by, say, 'August'.

With traditional typing, replacing July by August would create a problem as the number of letters (characters) is different. This does not matter with word processing systems as the text is formatted only on output. To output text from a disk, the operator needs to specify the width of the margins and other formatting details. In some cases, there is also the option to have right justification, i.e. the spacing in a line is chosen to ensure all lines end at the same distance across the page.

Spacing between the lines and paragraphs, the central-isation of headings and their underlining usually is specified when the text is input. The margins to be specified however depend upon the paper size and format to be used in a particular print run. Only at this stage can the word processor 'decide' where to break the sentences and start a new line. In doing this, the word processor will not split a word over two lines.

For a standard letter that is to be widely issued, one top copy will be produced on the printer and duplicated in the usual way. The operator can, however, request as many repetitive copies from the printer as necessary. The sophistication of the conventional word processing system allows extra facilities to be added at little marginal cost.

One natural extension of the basic word processing

centre is to allow satellite work stations to be connected. It is also an obvious step to provide a means of connecting a word processing centre to any main computer, via a standard telephone or data communication line.

Typical word processing applications

The basic characteristic of a word processor is the flexibility for retrieving and editing 'standard' text. This is an asset in two typical situations, the mass production of customised letters and the development of technical and commercial reports, specifications etc. over a protracted time.

The customised letter application for mailing shots and the like, draws upon the word processor's ability to insert minor changes into a standard letter held on file without having to retype each version. The simplest form of customisation would be for individual names and addresses read from one file to be added to a standard letter already held on a second file, or composed specially for this run. There can be many variations on this idea that allow a company using word processors to give a more personal service to their customers.

The second major area of application is for the production of reports and documents that go through several stages of revision and require the final stage to be error free. A typical example would be the production of legal documents, which using traditional methods would require a great deal of proof reading at each stage. In addition to legal documents, technical reports and specifications can benefit from a word processor's ability to change a word or phrase consistently throughout the text.

The scope for word processing can be illustrated by quoting some figures from an appraisal carried out by a chemical plant contractors.

A typical proposal (worth £10 million) would take six weeks to develop, from the receipt of enquiry to the issuing of a bid. Within this time period, the last week would be allocated for the formal writing up of the proposal. The proposal would consist of approximately 10,000 words consisting of:

Sales letter	1500 words
Financial terms	500 words
Legal terms	500 words
Technical description	6000 words
Miscellaneous	1500 words.

Anything from ten to twenty copies would be required for the final proposal.

Using a word processor would allow the sales letter, financial and legal terms to be customised variations of standard sections.

The bulk of these sections would not require as much checking as when they are typed from scratch each time. More attention could therefore be paid to the variations from standard. The ability of a word processor to edit readily existing textual files allows the technical description section to be started earlier.

A word processor helps to develop the written proposal in parallel with the project design and therefore obviates a full week being required for the final write-up. The resulting proposal is likely to be more accurate and produced earlier.

Optical Character Recognition (OCR)

Just as the speed of conventional computer applications is limited by input and output peripheral speeds, so word processors are limited by similar problems. The need to input text quickly into a word processor is a basic requirement if the ease of editing via a word processor is to be worthwhile. One possible approach to this is to use optical character readers.

Rough drafts are typed using an optical character fount and loaded into an optical character reader at up to fifty pages at a time. The reader can transfer up to 250 pages an hour directly into associated word processing equipment. The word processing station can therefore concentrate on the function it is specially suited to, the editing of the text. An installation, that previously had spent 75% of its time typing information into word processors, increased its throughput by 300% when it adopted OCR input.

Controlling a word processing system

The increased throughput and absence of conventional paperwork means that the office supervisor correspondingly needs to change to electronic methods for controlling the office.

Dealing with authors' and typists' queries and monitoring the work-in-progress requires the jobs to be logged electronically. A comprehensive microprocessor-based word management system allows all centralised dictation and word processed output to be logged automatically. Details of dictation brought in from pocket machines is entered via a VDU keyboard.

The VDU can display continuously an analysis of the word processing centre's current load under: being dictated; dictated but not yet assigned to typist; assigned for transcription; transcribed.

Specific information on up to 2000 current jobs can be screened to check on, originator's name, department, time received, type of work, length of job, typist assigned, etc. This information can be classified to produce lists of all work initiated by a particular individual, all work completed by a particular typist, etc. Daily, weekly or monthly reports can be produced of the work of the office.

15.3   Office output

Pneumatic tubes

The need to transfer physically paperwork or money within an organisation has led to microprocessor control being applied to the traditional pneumatic system. The traditional system only allowed traffic between two points; with a microprocessor-controlled unit diverting the carriers from the main ring to particular stations up to about sixty stations can be interconnected.

The required destination of a carrier is keyed in at the departure station. Up to a 2lb payload can be transferred, travelling at 30 mph.

Microfilm

The use of microfilm for convenient and high speed output from the computer is well established as COM (Computer Output on Microfilm). It is now being used as a means of helping to offset the workload imposed on word processing stations. Microprocessor-controlled microfilm equipment is capable of recording, storing and retrieving microfilms of data. The equipment can be linked to word processors such that the bulk of the paperwork input is microfilmed, and only the key data (customer name, account number, etc.) is entered into the word processor's CPU.

The microfilmed documentation is automatically indexed by the CPU and subsequently can initiate a microfilm search via the 'intelligent' microfilm reader.

15.4 An overview of the electronic office

The possible information flow from interrelating the methods and devices just discussed is shown in Figure 15.1. For completeness a videotex system has been included in the diagram. (Videotex was discussed in chapter 14.)

The description of a small business microcomputer system is given in the next section. It is not suggested that all these options would exist in any one office, the precise mix of equipment would depend upon the nature of the work undertaken.

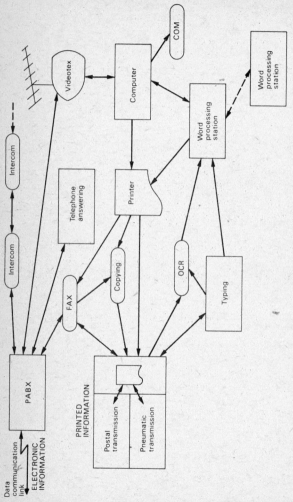

Figure 15.1 Information flow in an electronic office

An option not shown in Figure 15.1 is voice input/output. In some instances, the ability to enter commands and data by voice via a microphone would be an advantage. Continuing research into this method of input should ensure that such systems will be adopted. At present, the ability of the computer system to recognise reliably commands spoken by different people is limited due to unique variations in an individual's speech pattern. Voice input is currently restricted to applications where only a small number of staff use the system, i.e. stores, security doors, etc.

Voice output does not have these limitations. Software can cause the computer to synthesis vocabulary and string the words into appropriate phrases. Voice output is used to produce messages for transmission over telephone networks. For example, a stock level can be ascertained by telephone from a computer. Computer-originated messages also can guide a telephone user through a dialling sequence.

15.5 Small business systems

It is possible to buy a complete microcomputer system comprising a CPU, large typewriter keyboard, visual display unit (VDU), floppy disk unit and matrix printer for a few thousand pounds. This opens up the possibility of computerisation of business data to even the smallest company.

However, data processing requires software in the form of application packages in addition to the hardware listed above. These packages may be purchased commercially and were discussed in chapter 8, section 8.3.

An alternative approach is to employ an analyst/programmer to analyse, design and program systems specified by management. A typical file processing system is described below. This 'Contacts File' system was designed and programmed by some of the authors' specialist computing students as a final year project.

'Contacts File' system

The initial request for this system came from a user of an existing mainframe system, which was being used to maintain files of company names, addresses, telephone numbers and other coded details. This system was used for mailing information to companies on a selective basis and for reference purposes.

The main file of data on the existing system was held on one or more magnetic tapes, which were updated in batch mode. This entailed going through a number of steps including document preparation, batching of documents, punching and verification of data using paper tape, preparation and punching of suitable parameters, validation of data by computer program, a separate sort run to sequence the records in ascending contact number order, a separate run for updating the contacts file. This lengthy process meant that the information on the file was not always up to date, because data processing was delayed until a large enough batch had been prepared.

The new system that was requested needed to process data on-line, that is, by the operator interacting with the small business microcomputer system to be used. Direct access of data held on floppy disks was required for speedy amendment, insertion and deletion of records. Data entry was to be via the keyboard and validated on-line, so that it could be corrected immediately. The system had to be easy to understand and use, by providing prompts and error messages on the VDU and a user manual giving clear instructions.

The following description indicates some of the facilities that are available in the final implementation of the 'Contacts File' system. The complete system has many options and screen displays with prompt and error messages and is described in the systems report and user manual. The systems report contains full details of the background to the problem, file and record structures, program logic and displays. The user manual is very comprehensive and can be used as a training document for operators unfamiliar with the system. A shorter operating document is available for experienced operators.

```
                    SYSTEM MENU


                                          17/06/81


        1   SET DATE

        2   FILE MAINTENANCE

        3   FILE ENQUIRY

        4   SELECTIVE MAILING

        5   ALPHA LISTING

        6   FINISH


   WHICH JOB DO YOU WANT (1-6) ?  *
```

Table 15.1   Contacts file system menu

Various modules in the system are selected from the 'system menu' displayed on the VDU as shown in Table 15.1. For example, if FILE MAINTENANCE is selected by entering a 2 in the asterisk position, then the list shown in Table 15.2 is displayed. This module enables the operator to add, change or delete a record, and return to the system menu after the update so that a further option can be selected.

The operator is prompted to enter the data in the correct positions. The display in Table 15.2 starts as shown with rows of asterisks and with the flashing cursor in the first position, which varies according to the option selected. If a record is to be added to the file, the cursor is positioned on the first asterisk of the NAME data field; the

```
         CONTACTS FILE MAINTENANCE

                                    17/06/81
      C.NO.   *******
  01  NAME    ******************************
  02  POST    ******************************
  03  FIRM    ******************************
  04  ADD 1   ******************************
  05  ADD 2   ******************************
  06  ADD 3   ******************************
  07  TOWN    ******************************
  08  CNTY    ********************
  09  P/C     *********
  10  TEL     **********
  11  SIC     **
  12  SIZE    *
  13  Q.NO.   ****
  14  IRN     *****
  15  FIRM    ******************************
     (ALPHA)

  ADD/CHANGE/DELETE/END (A/C/D/E) ? *

  ALL CORRECT (Y/N) ? *
```

Table 15.2   Screen layout for adding, changing or
deleting a record

contact number is allocated automatically when the data
entry has been completed, before the record is written to
disk.

The asterisks indicate the maximum number of characters that may be entered for that data field. The asterisks
are replaced by the characters keyed in.

The operator presses a Return key at the end of each
data field and the remaining asterisks in that field are
eliminated. It is not necessary to provide data for every
field. When the operator has completed entry of the data
record, an option is provided for making changes to any of
the lines 01 to 15. Entering 00 allows the operator to get

out of the routine immediately if a change has been requested but is in fact not required.

Particular records can be requested for amendment or deletion. The operator is informed if the record is not on file, and is given the option of continuing or not. If the record is to be changed, the amended record is not written to the disk file (in its original place) until the operator has confirmed that the information is correct, in reply to a prompt. If the answer is N (no) then again the operator is asked which line is to be changed and the cursor is moved to that line. A record will not be deleted until the operator has replied Y (yes) to the prompt DELETE THIS RECORD (Y/N). An option is available for obtaining a hard copy on the printer of the changes that have been made to the file.

Additions are not allowed if the file is full, and a message FILE FULL is displayed on the screen. Changes and deletions can still be made at this stage.

Choosing ALPHA LISTING on the system menu gives a printed list of names and contact numbers in alphabetic order. Alternatively, self-adhesive labels can be printed for putting on to envelopes, if information needs to be sent out by post, by choosing SELECTIVE MAILING. The latter can also be used to give a list of names and addresses if ordinary printer stationery is used.

In both cases, the operator can indicate whether all the records on the file should be selected or whether records should be selected according to specified criteria. The operator can key in information to select companies which have a certain standard industrial classification (SIC), are of a certain size, are in a particular town or county. Single values or ranges may be specified and the selection is carried out on combination of criteria.

Another option is to make a file enquiry by contact number or name of company. The operator can key in a partial name, and all companies whose names start with the characters specified are displayed. Up to fifteen names are displayed at a time, and an option to continue or enter a contact number is then given. Entering a contact number displays that company's details; entering continue displays up to the next fifteen names. A message is displayed on the screen if no company is found that matches the partial name.

Alternatively, the operator can look up details of companies in the file which satisfy the criteria keyed in. These details are displayed on the screen and may be listed on the printer by requesting a hard copy.

The operator can also request a display or printout of how many companies in the file satisfy a combination of criteria which have been keyed in.

The prototype system comprised a suite of nine programs containing about 3500 BASIC instructions. The system is comprehensive and uses the typical file creation/ updating/interrogation procedures that are required for most small business applications.

Appendix A Answers to Exercises

1 11_{10}, 5_{10}, 50_{10}, 23_{10}, 186_{10}

2 11000_2, 11111_2, 1001110_2, 10011111_2

3

decimal	binary	decimal	binary
7	0111	7	0111
+ 4	+ 0100	+(−4)	+ 1100
11	1011	3	0011

decimal	binary	decimal	binary
4	0100	−4	1100
+(−7)	+ 1001	+(−7)	+ 1001
−3	1101	−11	0101

↑
sign bit
will be 1

4 20.375_{10}

5 1001.11_2

6 $0110\ 0010\ 0011\ 0111_{BCD}$

7 1583_{10}

8 DA_{16}

9 $100\ 010\ 011_2 = 423_8$

10

input signals			output signals	
A	B	C	sum	carry
0	0	0	0	0
0	1	0	1	0
0	0	1	1	0
0	1	1	0	1
1	0	0	1	0
1	1	0	0	1
1	0	1	0	1
1	1	1	1	1

11

		a	b	carry	sum	carry
half adder		1	1		0	1
full adder	1	1	1	1	1	1
full adder	2	1	0	1	0	1
full adder	3	0	1	1	0	1

$$7_{10} + 11_{10} = 18_{10} = 10010_2$$

Appendix B   ASCII Code (American Standard Code for Information Interchange)

bit 6 5 4	0 0 0	0 0 1	0 1 0	0 1 1	1 0 0	1 0 1	1 1 0	1 1 1
bit 3 2 1 0								
0 0 0 0	NUL	DLE	SP	0	@	P		p
0 0 0 1	SOH	DC1	!	1	A	Q	a	q
0 0 1 0	STX	DC2	"	2	B	R	b	r
0 0 1 1	ETX	DC3	#	3	C	S	c	s
0 1 0 0	EOT	DC4	$	4	D	T	d	t
0 1 0 1	ENQ	NAK	%	5	E	U	e	u
0 1 1 0	ACK	SYN	&	6	F	V	f	v
0 1 1 1	BEL	ETB	'	7	G	W	g	w
1 0 0 0	BS	CAN	(	8	H	X	h	x
1 0 0 1	HT	EM	)	9	I	Y	i	y
1 0 1 0	LF	SUB	*	:	J	Z	j	z
1 0 1 1	VT	ESC	+	;	K	[	k	{
1 1 0 0	FF	FS	,	<	L	\	l		
1 1 0 1	CR	GS	–	=	M	]	m	}
1 1 1 0	SO	RS	.	>	N	∧	n	~
1 1 1 1	SI	US	/	?	O	–	o	DEL

Characters are generally transmitted as 8-bit codes with the eighth bit giving even parity.

Some microcomputer systems provide two character sets, one of which has graphics symbols instead of the lower case letters.

Appendix C   Decimal, Binary, Hexadecimal and Octal numbers

decimal	binary	hexadecimal	octal
0	0000	0	0
1	0001	1	1
2	0010	2	2
3	0011	3	7
4	0100	4	4
5	0101	5	5
6	0110	6	6
7	0111	7	7
8	1000	8	10
9	1001	9	11
10	1010	A	12
11	1011	B	13
12	1100	C	14
13	1101	D	15
14	1110	E	16
15	1111	F	17

Appendix D   Logic Symbols (IEEE and ANSI approved)

inverter gate —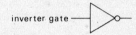

two input signals   multiple input signals

OR gate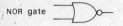

NOR gate

AND gate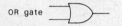

NAND gate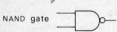

XOR gate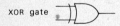

XNOR gate

Appendix E Glossary of Terms

This list of terms is not meant to provide an exhaustive dictionary definition, but to provide an *aide memoire* to terms previously met in the text.

accumulator	A storage location in which arithmetic results are accumulated
A/D converter	Analog to digital converter
address	The identification of a specific location in store
ADE	Angular Digital Encoder
AI	Artificial Intelligence
AM	Amplitude Modulation
ANSI	American National Standards Institute
ASCII	American Standard Code for Information Interchange
ASL	Arithmetic shift left
bar code	An optically read code consisting of a succession of printed lines where the encoding is by means of the line width and spacing
BASIC	Beginners All-purpose Symbolic Instruction Code – a high level programming language
Baudot code	A 5-bit telegraph code
BCD	Binary Coded Decimal
bit	An abbreviation of binary digit

bubble memory	A microelectronic serial access memory device in which the presence of a magnetic domain (bubble) represents a 1, the absence of a bubble 0
buffer	A temporary storage area for data established between two units of a system to allow for the different operating speeds of the units
bus	A route that carries signals from several sources to several destinations
byte	A group of binary digits, usually eight bits
CAI	Computer Aided Instruction
CAL	Computer Assisted Learning
CBL	Computer Based Learning
CCD	A Charge-Coupled Device used as a serial access memory
CCITT **Alphabet No 2**	A 5-bit telegraph code standardised by the International Telegraph and Telephone Consultative Committee
CET	The Council for Education Technology
character	A particular symbol in a set represented by a unique code of bits, e.g. letters of the alphabet, punctuation marks, numerals 0 to 9
chip	A single semi-conductor-based device normally containing an integrated circuit
clock	An electronic device that produces regular pulses enabling the operation of the

	units of a computer based system to be synchronised
CML	Computer Managed Learning
CMOS	Complementary MOS field-effect transistor
CNC	Computer Numerical Control
COBOL	COmmon Business Oriented Language, a high level programming language
COM	Computer Output on Microfilm
compiler	A program used to convert a high level language to machine code
control unit	That part of a computer that accesses program instructions, interprets them and initiates the appropriate action
CPU	Central Processing Unit
cross-assembler	A program used to translate an assembly language program on a different computer from the one on which it is to be executed
cross-compiler	A program used to translate a high level language program on a different computer from the one on which it is to be executed
cross talk	A form of interference where a signal in one circuit produces an unwanted signal in an adjacent circuit
cyclic binary code	A binary code where the bit pattern only changes by one bit in moving to an adjacent number
D/A converter	Digital to analog converter

decoder	A device that converts coded data into the required form
DIP	Dual In-line Package used for integrated circuits which has output pins arranged in two parallel lines
disk	A magnetic backing storage device which has information stored on concentric tracks over the surface of the disk
DMA	Direct Memory Access
DMAC	Direct Memory Access Controller
EAN	European Article Numbering system
EAROM	Electrically Alterable Read-Only Memory
EGR **valve**	Exhaust Gas Recirculation valve
EIA	Electronics Industry Association
emulator	A microprocessor system that functions in the same way as the actual microprocessor to be used
encoder	A device that converts data into the required coded form
EPROM	Erasable Programmable Read-Only Memory
FAMOS	Floating-gate Avalanche-injection Metal-Oxide Semi-conductor
FAX	Associated with a facsimile device or process
FET	Field Effect Transistor
fibre optics	An optical system that uses glass fibre as a light guide to transmit optical images or encoded light pulses

flag	An item of information (usually a bit) that indicates the condition of a related item of information, e.g. error flag, status flag
flip-flop	A bi-stable circuit that can be in, and remain in, one of two states depending upon the last input signal
floppy disk	A form of single pliable disk storage usually contained in a protective sleeve
FM	Frequency Modulation
FORTH	A high level programming language designed for use with small computers
FORTRAN	FORmulae TRANslation, a high level programming language
FSK	Frequency Shift Keying, a form of modulation
gate	In digital circuits, a circuit that has one or more inputs whose conditions determine the voltage level of the output
Gray code	A form of cyclic binary code
Hamming code	An error checking code, named after its inventor, that in some instances, can also be error correcting
hardware	The physical items and devices making up a system as opposed to the software (q.v.)
hex	Hexadecimal, a notation of numbers to the base 16, the sixteen digits usually being represented by 0–9 and A–F

high level	Applied to a programming language in which each instruction corresponds to several machine code instructions
IC	Integrated Circuit (q.v.)
ICE	In-Circuit Emulator, a device that can be plugged into the microprocessor socket of a prototype to emulate the proposed microprocessor
IEEE-**488**	An interface standard developed by the Institute of Electrical and Electronic Engineers
integrated circuit	A circuit manufactured as a single package, a monolithic integrated circuit has all the circuit components manu-factured into and on a chip of semi-conductor material
interface	The channels and associated circuitry allowing the con-nection between two electronic units, particularly a central processor and peripheral devices
interpreter	A program that translates high level programming instructions into machine code instructions which are immediately executed
IP	Information Providers, e.g. the providers of information in a videotex system
laser	Light Amplification by Stimulated Emission of Radiation

LED	Light Emitting Diode
LSI	Large Scale Integration (of ICs)
LVDT	Linear Variable Differential Transformer
machine code	The coding system adopted in the design of the central processor to represent the instruction set
magnetic stripe	A stripe of magnetisable material that can be encoded and read in a similar way to magnetic tape
mask	In microelectronics, the device used to shield selected areas of a semi-conductor chip during manufacture
memory	A device or circuit from which information can be retrieved (read-only memory) or to which information can be passed, stored and retrieved (read-addressable memory)
microfiche	Microfilm mounted as a slide rather than retained in roll film form
modem	A device that modulates out-going signals and demodulates incoming signals
modulation	A technique whereby a carrier frequency is modified in frequency or amplitude according to the characteristics of the signal to be conveyed, the original signal is obtained again by demodulation
MOS	Metal-Oxide Semi-conductor
MOSFET	A MOS Field Effect Transistor

multiplexing The simultaneous transmission of several signals through a common circuit

Murray code A 5-bit telegraph code

NC Numerical Control (of machine tools)

NMI Non-Maskable Interrupt, i.e. an interrupt that cannot be disabled

object program The program in machine code, produced from a high level or assembly language program by means of a compiler or an assembler

OCR Optical Character Recognition

octal A numbering system that uses 8 as a base

op code Operation code which specifies the particular operation to be performed by the control unit of a computer

PABX Private Automatic Branch Exchange

package A supplied program and associated documentation

PAM Pulse-Amplitude Modulation

parity check A check made on a group of bits by adding up the 1s present

PCB Printed Circuit Board

PCM Pulse Coded Modulation

PFM Pulse Frequency Modulation

photodetector Electronic devices that respond to light energy, e.g. photodiode, phototransistor, photocell

PIC Priority-Interrupt Controller

piezoelectric Pertaining to the effect of the

	electric charge produced when certain materials are stressed, the effect is reversible
PILOT	A high level authoring language used in CAL
PIO	Programmable parallel Input-Output device
PLL	Phase Locked Loop circuit
POS	Point of sale terminal
PROM	Programmable Read-Only Memory
protocol	The standard and format being followed in transmitting signals between two devices
RAM	Random Access Memory (read-addressable memory)
repeater	A device that transmits onwards, usually after amplification, any signals received
ROM	Read-Only Memory
RS232C	An interface standard
s100	A bus standard
sector	An angular portion of a disk file
semi-conductor	A material having a resistivity between a conductor and an insulator dependent upon its operating conditions
software	Programs and associated routines used by computer hardware
SOS	Silicon On Sapphire semi-conductor, a particular type of CMOS
source program	A program as originally written before being compiled or interpreted
stack	A series of memory locations

	used on a last in- first out (LIFO) basis
subroutine	A group of program instructions which can be entered from several points of the program, after execution control returns to the program routine which called the subroutine
TDM	Time Division Multiplexing
telecommunication	The transmission of signals over radio and other links involving great distances
Teletex	The transmission of digitally encoded information over television broadcasting channels
telesoftware	The provision of software by means of teletex
terminal	An input-output device in a computer system
transducer	Any device that converts a non-electrical parameter into electrical signals, or vice-versa
UART	Universal Asynchronous Receiver-Transmitter
UPC	Universal Product Code
USART	Universal Synchronous and Asynchronous Receiver-Transmitter
VDU	Visual Display Unit
Videotex	The transmission of digitally encoded information that can be displayed on modified television sets
wand	The name given to a hand held 'pen' that is passed over

	bar coded or magnetic stripe labels
Winchester disk	A hard disk unit sealed into a cartridge type case, used as an alternative to floppy disks
word	The number of bits that is handled by a computer in a single step

Appendix F   Suggested Further Reading

Books

General

Osborne, A, *An Introduction to Microcomputers, Vol 1 Basic Concepts*, Osborne & Associates, 1976.
Scientific American, *Microelectronics*, W H Freeman, 1977.

Logic circuits and number systems

Gosling, P E and Laarhoven, Q L M, *Codes for Computers and Microprocessors*, Macmillan, 1980.
Lewin, D, *Logical Design of Switching Circuits*, Nelson, 1974.
Malvino, A P, *Digital Computer Electronics*, McGraw-Hill, 1977.

Microprocessor structure, functions and interfacing

CBM, *Professional Computer User Manual*, Commodore Business Machines, 1979.
Dollhoff, T, *16-Bit Microprocessor Architecture*, Reston Publishing Co, 1979.
Lesea, A and Zaks, R, *Microprocessor Interfacing Techniques*, Sybex, 1977.

Programming

Barden, W, *How to Program Microcomputers*, Howard W Sams, 1977.

Colin, A, *Programming for Microprocessors*, Newnes-Butterworths, 1979.

Foster, C C, *Programming a Microcomputer: 6502*, Addison-Wesley, 1978.

Nichols, E A, Nichols, J C and Rony, P R, *Z-80 Microprocessor Programming & Interfacing*, Howard W Sams, 1979.

Carter, L R and Huzan, E, *Computer Programming in BASIC*, Teach Yourself Books, Hodder and Stoughton, 1981.

Parkin, A, *COBOL for students*, Edward Arnold, 1975.

Radford, A S, *Computer Programming/FORTRAN*, Teach Yourself Books, Hodder and Stoughton, 1975.

Welsh, J and Elder, J, *Introduction to Pascal*, Prentice-Hall, 1979.

MicroFORTHPrimer, FORTH Incorporated, 1978.

Instrumentation

Kantrowitz, P, Kousourou, G and Zuker, L, *Electronic Measurements*, Prentice-Hall, 1979.

Mansfield, P H, *Electrical Transducers for Industrial Measurement*, Butterworths, 1973.

Woolvet, G A, *Transducers in Digital Systems*, Peter Peregrinus, 1977.

Systems development and applications

Motorola Semiconductor Products, *M6800 Applications Manual*, Motorola, 1975.

Ogdin, C A, *Microcomputer Management and Programming*, Prentice-Hall, 1980.

Race, J, *Computer-Based Systems*, Teach Yourself Books, Hodder and Stoughton, 1977.

Simons, G L, *Robots in Industry*, NCC Publications, 1980.

Journals

The following journals contain news items and articles on microcomputer products, programming and applications, as well as book reviews and in some instances details of microcomputer user groups and clubs.

Byte
Compute
Computer Bulletin
Computer Journal
Computer Weekly
Computing
Computing Today
Educational Computing
Electronics Today,
    International
Journal of Microcomputer
    Applications
Micro Journal
Personal Computer World
Personal Computing
Practical Computing
Which Computer
Wireless World
Your Computer
Infomatics

Index